William Burton

The Use of Lead Compounds in Pottery

from the Potter's Point of View

William Burton

The Use of Lead Compounds in Pottery
from the Potter's Point of View

ISBN/EAN: 9783337846756

Printed in Europe, USA, Canada, Australia, Japan

Cover: Foto ©Andreas Hilbeck / pixelio.de

More available books at **www.hansebooks.com**

The use of Lead Compounds in Pottery,

from the Potters' Point of View.

By WILLIAM BURTON, F.C.S.

(Director of Pilkington's Tile & Pottery Co. Ltd.)

By request of the Joint Committee of the Allied Manufacturers' Associations of Great Britain.

LONDON:
SIMPKIN, MARSHALL, HAMILTON, KENT & CO. LTD.
4, STATIONERS' HALL COURT, E.C.
1899.

MANCHESTER :

Printed by CHORLTON & KNOWLES, Mayfield Press.

1899.

CONTENTS.

I. An Outline of the Processes of Pottery Manufacture.

II. The Sources of Danger.

III. Existing Official Regulations at Home and Abroad.

IV. The Statistics of Plumbism—What They Show and What They Do Not Show.

V. The Report of Professors Thorpe and Oliver.

Appendix A. Plumbism and the Workmen's Compensation Act.

Appendix B. H. J. Tennant, M.P., and the Case against Arbitration.

Appendix C. The Official Regulation of the Pottery Industry at Home and Abroad.

NOTE.

THIS is, in great measure, a controversial pamphlet, but, I hope, none the less fair and accurate on that account. The reckless and sensational statements made in public speeches and in the press during the last twelve months or so about the pottery manufacturers and their doings, were ill calculated to bring about a satisfactory result. The evils of lead poisoning are far too real and serious to be treated in the rhetorical, even hysterical method adopted by our critics. They present a series of scientific problems ; none the less simple because the malady is so insidious, and our processes so variable and intricate; which demand for their solution the most rigorous and exact examination. This little essay forms an attempt to regard the question solely from such a point of view. Every effort has been made to render the information contained as exact and complete as possible. All the figures quoted are taken from official sources. Wherever a statement has been made regarding matters of fact, it has been expressed in such a form as to be beyond dispute. The sole idea underlying this essay has been that of making a real contribution to the discussion, by an examination of all the suggestions and criticisms emanating from authoritative sources.

My thanks are due to manufacturers and others for information and suggestions. In this connection I must mention Messrs. F. Rawdon Smith, John Ridgway, R. Jamieson, H. Watkin, and W. Jackson. I am still more indebted to my brother and co-worker, Joseph Burton, for many valuable suggestions, and for the care he has taken in revising the sheets for the press.

WILLIAM BURTON.

Clifton Junction,
   Near Manchester.
     May 1st, 1899.

Wherever the word " Report " is used the reference is to the Report of Professors Thorpe and Oliver on " the use of lead compounds in pottery."

A Brief Account
of Pottery Processes.

It is difficult for a potter to realise how little knowledge is possessed about his special business, even by the most intelligent of outsiders. What the potter frequently takes for gross misstatements on the part of his critics, are often stumbling efforts due to imperfect knowledge of a highly specialised trade. When writers in the press and public speakers use statements implying that "pottery manufacture is a dangerous trade in all its branches," and at the same time infer that every worker on a pottery is a "potter," or that every worker runs risks of "plumbism," the potter who understands his business is very apt to be contemptuous of the statements made by those who have evidently such little knowledge of the practical details on which the vital questions of "dust" and "plumbism" turn. Such misapprehensions are unfortunate, as they render improvement difficult. Our first endeavour therefore shall be to simplify some of the difficulty presented to the outsider.

There are few, if any, industries that are at once so extensive and yet so detailed and intricate as "Pottery." From a brick to a painted china vase, from the commonest roofing tile to decorative or constructive faience, and from the huge slabs made for lavatory conveniences to the small fittings connected with delicate electrical appliances, everything made of clay is classed under the general and comprehensive term "Pottery." Some manufacturers produce goods of one class only, while others produce, on one works, a considerable variety. It is evident from the foregoing that regulations which would be wise, suitable and efficient for one branch of such an industry, might be quite impossible of application or inefficient in some other branch. The risks are not only very unevenly distributed over the different works according to the special business of each works, but in every works the risks are very unevenly distributed among the different groups of workers.

The sub-division of labour and the applications of machinery have been carried to such an extent in the industry as a whole during the last century and a half, that a factory producing goods of only one class, will contain many groups of occupations which differ from each other in their influence on the health of the workpeople, quite as much as if they were distinct and separate industries.* If this be true of a works where goods of one kind only are manufactured, the conditions of a manufactory producing china, earthenware and tiles, or any similar mixture of products, must be complicated in the extreme, yet there are many works in England in which the latter set of conditions exists.

It would be a weary and a profitless task to describe for the outsider all the separate processes employed in the Pottery industry, but it may simplify what follows and render it easier of comprehension if we briefly review the main processes connected with the production of earthenware: say the ware used for ordinary domestic purposes.

In the first place, potter's clay is not ordinary clay used just as it is dug from the pit. Every kind of potter's clay is a more or less complex mixture of substances. For earthenware the mixture contains at least four ingredients, (1) Ball clay, a plastic clay; (2) China clay, a white clay; (3) Ground, calcined flint; (4) Ground Cornish stone.

The exact composition of such a body varies with each manufactory, because the mixture suitable for the production of ordinary earthenware differs widely from that known as granite ware, both these differ again from the clay used in making large sanitary ware pieces, and so on through the whole range of earthenware production; there is no help for it, as the working qualities of each kind of potter's clay must be adapted to his special requirements. The body mixture once obtained, is the foundation of the whole business, for it controls the firing of the ovens and kilns, the composition of the glaze, &c. In

*See on this point "The Diseases of Occupations," by J. T. Arlidge, M.D., p. 310, par. 1

a word the details of a potter's business all hang together—disturb one, you disturb all the rest; and the body is the foundation.

Enginemen, Millmen, Sliphousemen and their Attendants.

The calcining and grinding of the flints, the grinding of the Cornish stone, and the mixing up of the raw clays with water, and then the compounding of these ingredients in determined proportions, and the cleansing and preparation of the mixture, so as to fit it for use by the operative potter, find employment for a considerable amount of labour, which is free from any special risk.

This labour is almost exclusively performed by adult males.

Operative Potters and their Attendants.

The clay thus prepared is passed on to the workers who have to shape it. Only the workers in this branch are known technically as " Potters." The shaping may be done by a variety of processes, Throwing, Pressing, Casting, Jolly and Jigger work, &c., &c. The modern tendency is for these processes to be further subdivided, so that each worker performs only one kind of work, and often only one step in the complete shaping process.

When the ware has been shaped, it is finished by smoothing the surfaces of the article, and by trimming and smoothing its edges or seams. These proceedings, the exact details of which vary according to the particular kind of ware, or the manufacturing processes, create a certain amount of dust.* This dust is of course a mixed mineral dust, almost as injurious when breathed, say, as the dust made by stonecutters, but it is not in any sense a poisonous dust.

The removal of such dust is already provided for by Rule 3 of 1894, and by Rule 6 of the Special Rules of 1898 (see Appendix C. p. 70.)

---

* In many processes of "fettling" the ware, it is trimmed while still moist. In such cases, of course, no dust is created.

"Biscuit" Oven Placers and Firemen.

When the piece of ware has been thus finished, so far as its clay state is concerned, it is completely dried in hot-air stoves, and passed on to the "sagger" house connected with the ovens. Here it is placed in "saggers" or fireclay boxes to protect it from the direct impact of the flames: and the "saggers" are piled in the oven, where the pottery receives its first (or "Biscuit") fire.

The operations of placing and firing, though in themselves laborious, contain no elements of danger, except such as usually attend severe manual labour.

During the firing of the oven, the fireman and his assistants have to bear exposure to considerable heat for periods of from twenty minutes to half-an-hour at a time, but the work is not to be compared in intensity to that of the drivers and stokers of locomotive engines, puddlers, steel smelters, glass-blowers, or of many similar groups of operatives in other callings.

Biscuit sorting and Warehousing.

When the ware is drawn from the biscuit oven it is carried to the sorting room and examined for defects. It is then sorted into grades, and carried into the biscuit warehouses to be stored till required.

The operations of biscuit sorting are almost invariably performed by women and young girls. The carrying and stacking in the warehouses almost invariably by youths and men. There are no special risks in these branches of the trade.

Printers, Transferers and their Assistants.

Ware, which requires printing, is taken into the printing shops, where it is printed with special mineral pigments, very few of which contain any lead (at all events of those used at this stage of the process). As the pigments used are mixed

Printers, Transferers and their Assistants. continued.

with boiled oil into a stiff printers' ink, it is difficult to see that any special danger can arise to the
printers who print the colours, or to the transferers* (always women and girls) who transfer
these prints on to the ware.

Dippers and their Assistants.

When the ware has been printed, and the oily
matter burnt out of the prints, or without being
printed at all, as the case may be, it is taken into
the dipping house. The dipper's business is to
coat the piece with a layer of glaze, by plunging it
into a bath, containing the finely ground glazing
materials in suspension in water.

As this is the first of the dangerous sections of
the trade we give such figures as are available as
to the number of workers employed. The most
complete available figures are those collected by
the Home Office relating to the Staffordshire potteries,† where it is estimated that two-thirds of the
total number of persons employed in the industry
are gathered together.

In July, 1898, the following numbers were employed:—

Dippers.— 9 males under 18, 15 females under
18, 486 adult males, 66 adult females.

Dippers' Assistants.—415 males under 18, 49
females under 18, 103 adult males, 58 adult females.

Ware Cleaners after Dippers.

When the ware has been dipped, it is passed on
to the ware cleaners, who examine the pieces to see
that they are properly dipped, and remove all superfluous glaze by scraping with a knife, or by other
suitable means. This of course creates dust, and as
this dust contains lead compounds it is essential
that such dust, wherever it is created, *i.e.* wherever

* That is assuming they are not also colour dusters (q. v.)
† For complete table see page 24.

Ware Cleaners after Dippers. continued.

the glaze is trimmed " dry," should be effectually removed from the face of the worker.

As this occupation is a light one, it is usually performed by women, and occasionally by young persons. The table already quoted from furnishes us with the following particulars :-

Ware Cleaners, 15 males under 18, 76 females under 18, 90 adult males and 382 adult females.

Glost Placers.

The next process is to place the ware thus coated with glaze and cleaned, in another set of "saggers" for the firing necessary to melt the glaze. This occupation is very largely performed by adult males, but there are certain sections of the industry, in which, from the small size of many of the articles manufactured, the work can be much better and more quickly performed by women and young persons. No one in this country, we believe, would think of employing women or young persons for the placing of large or heavy articles (though such a system largely prevails on the Continent), but it is obvious that for the placing of small electric fittings, of tiles so small that 600 or 900 go to a square yard, and of many similar articles which are made in enormous quantities, the work is far better suited to the nimble fingers of women and young persons than it is to those of adult males. There can be no doubt that the great majority of women and young persons employed in this country as glost placers, are employed in placing the small articles above mentioned.* We extract the following figures from the table previously used:-

Glost Placers, 58 males under 18, 8 females under 18, 1747 adult males, 38 adult females.

Majolica Paintresses and Glaze Blowers.

In certain branches of the general earthenware trade, but not those connected with the production of dinner, toilet and sanitary goods, glazes are also

* Women placers in this country only place the articles in saggers, they do not carry them to the ovens.

Tunstall,

With Compliments from

Arthur P. Llewellyn,

Secretary.

**Majolica
Paintresses
and Glaze
Blowers.
continued.**

applied, not by dipping, but by painting or some similar process.

These workers are almost exclusively women, thus, in the two classes here mentioned, we find in the table

Majolica Paintresses, 62 females under 18, 233 adult females No males.

**Glost Sorters
and
Warehousemen.**

Glaze and Colour Blowers, 9 adult males, 12 adult females.

When the glaze has been fired the ware is again sorted and warehoused. These occupations find employment for a considerable number of people, but we need not consider them further.

A large amount of ware is however decorated by applying colours, enamel colours as they are called, on to the surface of the fired glaze. The colours or metals used for such purposes consist of mineral pigments fluxed with a large proportion of lead compounds, so that when they are exposed to a very moderate fire, the melting of these fluxes will fuse the colour into the surface of the previously fired glaze.

These colours may be applied by groundlayers, colour dusters, onglaze printers, enamel paintresses, painters and gilders.

**Groundlayers
and
Colour dusters.**

These operatives, after coating the fired and glazed ware with oil, dust over it enamel colours. In these occupations, therefore, the difficulty again arises, that a certain amount of dust containing deleterious compounds is created. The first essential precaution therefore is the effective removal of such dust from the face of the worker. These are generally the most dangerous of all the specified employments. The numbers employed are given as follows:—

Groundlayers, 9 females under 18, 89 adult males, 373 adult females.

Colour Dusters, 24 females under 18, 7 adult males, 118 adult females.

Enamel Paintresses, Painters, Gilders. These operatives use very much the same materials as those used by groundlayers and colour dusters, but as the colours or metals are in these processes mixed with "fat" oils and applied with brushes, the occupations do not involve risk of plumbism.

In addition to the occupations thus specifically mentioned which are all met with in one section of the industry, there are many subsidiary departments, but we have mentioned all which involve risks from dust, either containing lead or otherwise.

In works other than earthenware works, there are other processes, but they need not be specified here, as they either closely resemble those described above, or are not germane to our present considerations.

Leaving aside the question of clay dusts, as these are already efficiently dealt with in existing Home Office regulations, we can now single out the workers who come into contact with lead compounds. These comprise dippers, dippers' assistants, ware cleaners, glost placers, majolica paintresses, glaze blowers, groundlayers, colour dusters, &c. These are the workers exposed to the possibility of plumbism.

It is evident however, that they are not all equally exposed.

(a) Because the substances they use vary greatly in the amount of lead compounds they contain, and consequently vary proportionately in their toxic intensity.

(b) Because in some of these occupations the conditions are more favourable to the taking of lead compounds into the system than in others.

Both these considerations are of the utmost importance, and they explain at once the wide divergences known to exist between different sets of workers.

All the dangerous substances used may be divided into three groups, according to the degree of fire used in fixing them on to the ware.

Easy Fire.	Enamel Colours	-	20 to 50 p.c. of lead oxide.
	Jet & Rockingham Glazes	40 to 60	,, ,,
	Majolica Glazes	-	25 to 50 ,, ,,

Medium Fire	Earthenware Glazes		14 to 22 p.c. of lead oxide.
	Sanitary ware ,,		
	Granite ,, ,,		

Full Fire - China Glazes - 10 to 15 p.c. of lead oxide.

The figures in the foregoing table represent the percentage of lead oxide contained generally in the substances specified. The less lead a colour or a glaze contains the more fire it will need for its fusion. This is a very different statement from the one frequently made, that potters use lead to save coal. The firing temperature is not fixed to accommodate a certain percentage of lead ; *the proportion of lead, or of other fluxes, is fixed by the temperature of firing,* and that is decided by many intricate considerations, such as the nature of the body (or of the fired glaze in dealing with enamel colours), the temperature at which the ware can be fired in biscuit or glost without ruinous loss, and last, but by no means least, the fugitive nature of many of the colouring bases at the potter's disposal.

It is evident from the foregoing tabular statement, which is a sufficiently accurate approximation for our purposes, that other things being equal, China glazes have the least toxic intensity, while Enamel colours, Jet and Rockingham and Majolica glazes come at the other end of the scale in this respect.

In addition to the question of **amount** of lead compounds in any particular mixture comes the question of its **condition,** but as in these substances it is common in English practice to use white lead for the glazes, and an almost equally soluble silicate or borosilicate as the flux for enamel colours, this is not a consideration of great moment.

Beyond the question of toxic intensity however, there is the equally important consideration of the nature of the process. In ground-laying, colour dusting, and ware cleaning, the operations necessarily produce dust, and as, in the past, sufficient attention has not been paid to the removal of such dust, we find these occupations showing the largest percentage of plumbic cases among all those specified. In dipping and majolica painting, the danger does not arise so much from the creation of dust, as from the fact that the fingers of the majolica paintresses and the hand and sometimes the forearm of the dippers become coated with the glazing liquid. Unless care is taken, by keeping a sponge and clean water close at hand, to wash this off frequently, a thin cake of dry glaze gathers on the fingers, whence it is readily conveyed to the lips, face, or nostrils, by putting the fingers to the mouth, nose, or eyes. With glost placers, who have the lowest attack rate of all the workers in lead, the risk is so slight that with ordinary care on the part of the operatives it might be abolished altogether. Indeed, it is a question if plumbism exists among glost placers at all, except in certain branches of the trade, where the placers are, to a limited extent, also ware cleaners.

To sum up :—A statement was made in the *Manchester Guardian* in one of its articles on " Lead poisoning in the Potteries," that from official figures there were 70,873 people employed in 1896 in the pottery industry in the United Kingdom, of which number 46,568 or about two-thirds of the whole were employed in the Potteries district of Staffordshire. Knowing, as we do, that this district produces nearly every form of pottery produced in the Kingdom, we may take the official figures as given in the Report of Professors Thorpe and Oliver for this particular district as typical of the industry as a whole. Assuming that the total number employed was the same in 1898 as in 1896, we find that in the latter year, the number of persons employed in all the processes entailing risk of plumbism, amounted to 3,123 males of all ages, and 1,580 females of all ages, a total of 4,703 workers. So that, in round numbers, we may say one worker in every 10 employed in the pottery works of Staffordshire runs some risk of " plumbism." Taking the highest number of reported cases in the three years during which compulsory notification has been in force, we find 386 reported cases in 1897. This gives us the further fact that among 4,703 workers, 386 cases of plumbism were reported in the worst year yet known. The exact significance of these figures will be dealt with in the section dealing with the official statistics as a whole (see p. 22).

We find then that in the Pottery industry generally, one operative in every ten runs some risk of lead poisoning, and that of the

10 per cent so exposed there is one reported case of plumbism among every twelve workers. Whether the cases are slight or serious there is no evidence to show. If a worker is so slightly affected as to be kept away from work for three days or a week, it is a case, in the returns, equally with the most serious attack imaginable. There is also no evidence to show what proportion of these cases are attacks of fresh persons, and what proportion are fresh attacks of persons who have been attacked once and have been allowed to resume work by **their own medical man.** What we do know is that the number of fatal cases is not, as has been generally assumed, a large percentage of those actually attacked.

We have now to consider the question of the means that ought to be taken to cope with such a state of affairs, which, after every consideration that can be reasonably urged in mitigation, is still serious enough to demand every practical effort for its removal on the part not merely of the Home Office, but of manufacturers and operatives too.

———————

II. The Sources of Danger.

The greatest enemy to the health of the operative, in those branches of the pottery industry which contain any element of special danger at all, is **Dust**. When that dust contains a considerable proportion of lead compounds, the danger is greatly intensified. The first condition, therefore, which appeals to anyone possessing an efficient acquaintance with the present conditions of the industry, is " How best to deal with the various processes in which dust is produced." The means that can be adopted to this desirable end may be classified, for convenience, under certain heads.

1. The diminution where practicable of the amount of dust created.

In certain parts of the pottery industry, this has already been done to a very considerable extent, as the evidence of medical men shows that the disease known as "potter's asthma," once as great an evil in the " Potteries " as plumbism, is far less prevalent than it was some forty or fifty years ago. This may be partly due to the better food and the greater sobriety of operative potters as a class, but much of the improvement must be attributed to the improved conditions existing in the workshop. These improved conditions have been largely brought about by the manufacturers themselves without pressure from the outside.

In other directions, however, modern methods have led to the production of great numbers of articles from potter's clay, not in a wet or plastic state at all, but reduced to the condition of dust. The grinding of such dust, and its making up into tiles and other articles, as well as the modern method of finishing earthenware, which is known as "towing," has operated in a precisely opposite direction. In dealing, therefore, with this question, we must remember that modern developments have led, and appear likely in the future to lead to the greater production of clay dust, and we come therefore to the second of our precautionary measures.

2. The removal of dust, of whatever kind, as rapidly and perfectly as possible from the face of the worker.

This consideration really goes to the root of the whole matter, for whether the dust be the dust unavoidably produced in the process of tile making, earthenware towing, china placing, and china scouring, or the more deleterious dust containing lead compounds, produced in ware cleaning after the dipper, in ground laying, colour dusting, or glaze blowing, the evil may, to a very great extent, be remedied by the provision of means for effectual removal of such dust from the face of the worker. In this respect the potter, like every other worker in an old established industry, has to contend against the traditions of the trade, and the customs of his ancestors. In every pottery, however, in the United Kingdom, the Home Office rules of 1898 render it imperative that efficient means shall be employed to remove the dust in all places and processes where it is necessarily created. We are, therefore, justified in the conclusion that the evils of dust are now recognized by the manufacturers as well as the Home Office, and it only remains for the operatives to see that no carelessness or inattention on their part shall mar the beneficial operations of the rules already in force.

The efficient removal of dust, while in itself a sufficient protection in some of the occupations, must, in others, such as those of dippers, dippers' assistants, majolica paintresses, &c., who use glazes in a liquid form, be strengthened by other regulations. The provision of adequate ventilation and the removal of such dust as is created from their workshops, will go only a little way towards removing the evils incident to such occupations. We have, therefore, to consider in this group of cases and in the case of all workers handling poisonous substances, what further precautions may be necessary in order to deal with them effectually.

Such further precautions as are dictated by the present state of our knowledge may be classified in the following manner :—

(A.) Where injurious or dangerous substances are used, to discover and to apply such combinations of them, as shall reduce their toxic power to the lowest practicable limit.

This point is fully considered from the potter's point of view in the section of this pamphlet which treats of the Home Office report on the use of lead, &c. (see p. 32).

(B.) By periodical medical examination, to withdraw from these occupations, two classes of operatives :—

(*a*) The persons constitutionally prone to contract plumbism, *i.e.* such persons as have a "scrofulous" taint, or have inherent tendency toward gout, rheumatism, etc.

(*b*) Those operatives who are so reckless and untidy in their habits that they **will** play with dangerous compounds, as if they were harmless.

(c.) By providing such washing and clothing conveniences as shall prevent the operatives from conveying dust containing lead compounds into their houses, or into the works' dining-rooms where they take their meals.

(D.) By educating all operatives in elementary ideas of cleanliness, and the proper care of their health and person.

It is proposed to deal in the next chapter with the existing Departmental regulations for enforcing the above mentioned considerations. The questions connected with Section (A) are treated separately (see p. 32), while consideration (D) is hardly a matter for the manufacturing potter, considering the enormous sums spent by the nation at large on its public elementary schools.

III. Existing Regulations in the United Kingdom and in Foreign Countries.

The Home Office has drawn up, and all Pottery manufacturers in this country are now working under, a series of regulations (unfortunately, the most important of them of very recent creation,) which deal with all the points raised in the previous chapter, except point No. 2. These regulations will be found, together with an earlier set of regulations out of which they sprung, printed in full as an Appendix, (Appendix C, page 69). It is not necessary therefore, to consider them in detail here, but their contents may be summarised as follows :—

1. No person under 14 years of age, and after August 1st, 1899, no person under 15 years of age, shall be employed in any dangerous process.

2. All women and young persons employed in the dangerous processes shall be examined once a month by the district certifying surgeon, who has the power to order their suspension from such employment, if he considers they show symptoms of plumbism. No person after such suspension is allowed to again work in any of the dangerous processes, without the written sanction of the certifying surgeon.

3. Provides that registers must be kept to record the above information.

4. The manufacturer must provide and maintain suitable overalls and head coverings for all women and young persons employed in such processes. These the manufacturer must keep in proper custody ; he must also see that all overalls are washed at least once a week. He must also provide a suitable place in which the above workers can deposit clothing put off during working hours.

5. No food or drink may be prepared or partaken of, and no person may remain during meal times in any room where such processes are carried on. The manufacturer must make suitable provision for the accommodation, during meal times, of persons employed in such places or processes.

6. In all processes the manufacturers must adopt efficient methods for the removal of dust.

8. The manufacturer must provide and maintain sufficient and suitable washing conveniences for all persons employed in the specified processes, and stringent, detailed regulations are inserted regarding the washing conveniences that must be provided.

The remaining regulations deal with the ventilation, sweeping, and cleansing of the workshops, or of the working appliances used.

The most valuable of these regulations, as regards the health of the operative, are undoubtedly those dealing with the various means for the removal of dust, and, most of all, the regulation for the monthly medical examination of certain classes of workers. It is frequently charged against manufacturers, by people who, from their positions, ought to know better, that not only have they done nothing in these directions themselves, but that when such regulations have been proposed, they have, either passively or actively, resisted their coming into operation.* So far from this being the truth, it is a fact that there is not a single important regulation in the Home Office rules of 1898, which had not been previously put into practice by manufacturers themselves.

Methods of ventilation and of removing dust, for instance, had been in use at many manufactories, years before such a regulation was imposed by the Home Office, and when the Home Office desired to make these regulations binding on the trade as a whole, its conclusions were based on the body of practical experience then existing among the pottery manufacturers themselves, on these very points. The most important point in the manufacturers favour is, however, the history of No. 2 rule of the 1898 regulations. This is the most valuable of all the rules yet enacted, as it provides for the monthly medical examination of all women and young persons employed in processes where lead compounds are used. The history of this rule is given in full in Appendix B, but we may just mention here that the application of such a rule was proposed by manufacturers themselves in 1895, and if the operatives have had to wait until this year for the rule to come into general operation, the fault does not lie with the manufacturers.

* See Appendix B.

Some manufacturers (again without waiting for the Home Office) adopted this monthly medical examination on their own account, and when the Home Office was preparing the rules of 1898, there existed a fund of valuable information obtained by manufacturers, to convince anyone who needed convincing, of the value of such a rule. Even then the Home Office only drafted the rule so as to cover women and young persons.

The efficacy of this particular rule in the directions shown on page 14, is the main cause of the gratifying decrease in the number of cases of plumbism reported in the first three months of this year, as compared with previous periods. We append the official return.

	1898*					1899			
	Jan.	Feb.	Mar.	Total		Jan.	Feb.	Mar.	Total
Pottery trades -	56	25	40	121	...	21	28	27	76
*Glass polishing	Included in Pottery.					2	1	4	7
Other trades -	72	53	61	186	...	72	101	90	263

Comparing the first three months of 1899 with the same period of 1898, the reported cases of plumbism from the pottery industry have **diminished** by over 33 per cent., while in other industries they have **increased** by over 41 per cent.

In the first quarter of 1898 there was no compulsory medical inspection in our industry, and where manufacturers had established such a scheme, the medical man could only advise, not suspend, the worker. In 1899 the examination had been in force for a few months throughout the country—long enough at all events to have produced a marked improvement. Further comment would be superfluous.

Having shown the excellent provisions that are now in force in this country, devised so as to diminish the evils connected with the manufacture of pottery, it is interesting to compare them with the regulations in force in foreign countries.

For this purpose, foreign countries may be divided into three groups:—

1. Countries in which wares are produced, based on English discovery and English practice.

2. Countries in which wares are produced, unlike those produced in England, but still entering into competition with them in the world's markets.

3. Countries whose manufactures are inconsiderable in amount, or do not compete with English goods.

To the first group of countries belong France, Germany, Belgium, Holland, Denmark, Sweden, Spain, and the United States of North America. In all these countries wares are made exactly on the lines of English earthenware, and by the methods and processes first developed in this country. Great efforts are also being made at the present time (in many cases by the help of State subsidies), to domicile in those countries other branches of the English pottery trade, such as the manufacture of sanitary goods.

To the second group of countries belong France, Germany, The Austrian Empire, and some other countries in so far as they produce hard-paste porcelains, and stonewares, which, while competing in certain markets with our own productions, are produced by practical methods very different from those used in this country; forming, in fact, a distinct branch of the pottery industry.

The countries of the third group include Switzerland and the smaller European States generally, which either produce an insufficient amount of pottery for their own requirements, or make certain special little manufactures which do not compete with English goods.

It is evident that the official regulations controlling these industries in the countries of the first two groups, and of the first group in particular, are of importance to the English potter, as one of the conditions of his commercial existence is, that he shall be able to compete in the world's markets—not merely in the home market—with the goods produced in those countries.

If, however, the regulations in force in any of the countries prescribe such conditions as to the use of certain substances as will impair the quality of the articles produced by its potters, it is obvious that such restrictions will place that group of potters at a serious commercial disadvantage.

The bearing of these points will be more readily understood when we deal with the question of leadless glazes, and the limitation of the proportions of lead compounds to be used by English potters, in the next chapter, (see p.p. 34 and 47).

Professors Thorpe and Oliver, in considering the question of the use of lead compounds in glazes, very wisely obtained from the Foreign Office and other official sources, information as to the rules and regulations imposed on the pottery industry in foreign countries. The information obtained by them is set out on pages 46 to 50 of their report.

For the convenience of our readers we print it in full in Appendix C of this pamphlet, but we may here briefly summarise it, as we have already summarised the existing English regulations.

FRANCE.

Although the attention of the Minister of Commerce and Industry has been repeatedly called to the effects of lead poisoning in potteries, it is thought that the risks of poisoning can be obviated by the strict observance of Article 6 of the Decree of 10th March, 1894, which, so far as it relates to the pottery industry, runs as follows :—

" Dust shall be drawn straight out of the workroom the instant it is produced."

" To deal with light dust, hoods with exhaust chimneys, or any equally good means of extraction, shall be put up."

" The air of the workroom shall be renewed from time to time, so that it remains in such a state of purity as is necessary for the health of the workpeople."

Compare such benevolent expressions of good intentions, unprovided, apparently, with any administrative machinery, with the elaborate and stringent regulations enforced on pottery manufacturers in this country, (see p. 15).

GERMANY.

The Imperial Government has made no special regulations for the manufacture of earthenware and china.

We are told that the President of Police in Berlin has made an order relating to the prevention of lead poisoning, but one fails to see the value of such a regulation, which does not apply in the least to the districts where earthenware is chiefly made in Germany. It is very much as if in this country a regulation should be formulated by the London County Council.

AUSTRIA.

No special regulations exist for protecting the health of the workers in the manufacture of china and earthenware.

Potteries, however, may not be opened or extended without an official certificate of authorization, showing that due provision has been made for the security and health of the workers liable to unhealthy influences.

The preliminary examination by competent authorities is required to be "particularly stringent."

This provision evidently corresponds in action to the ordinary Factory and Workshops Acts in force in this country. (See Section 75 of the Factory and Workshops Act, 41 Victoria, cap. 16.)

It must be observed further that there is no statement here as to what happens when once the works has been opened or extended, and apparently there is no further control over what takes place.

DENMARK, ITALY, NORWAY AND SWEDEN.

In these countries no special legislation exists for the protection of the health of workers engaged in the manufacture of china or porcelain.

BELGIUM.

No State regulations have been made.

HOLLAND.

Certain rules are in force, which are apparently on the lines of the general Factory Acts in this country, dealing with ventilation, the provision of sufficient working space, and such matters.

We are not informed that any special rules for the pottery industry are made or enforced by the Government, but it is stated that the large manufacturers have adopted certain regulations themselves for dealing with the dangerous branches of the trade.

UNITED STATES.

The Department of Labour states that there is no legislation, either State or National, especially directed to the giving of expert advice and assistance to manufacturers of pottery relative to the health of the operatives employed.

It seems rather futile after that, for the United States Department of Labour to add that the State of Louisiana (a State in which the pottery industry can hardly be said to exist) has given its Board of Health power to regulate dangerous trades.

SWITZERLAND.

Excellent instructions have been drawn up by the Inspector of Factories for persons working in all industries in which lead compounds are used.

There is no evidence to show that these instructions are acted upon, and the naïve remark is made that "the pottery industry is not very extensive in Switzerland."

A perusal of the foregoing precis of the steps taken in the various civilised countries for dealing with the difficulties connected with the manufacture of pottery shows conclusively that England has already enforced regulations which far exceed in extent, stringency and minuteness of detail, those enforced in any State or country of Europe or America.

We are not dealing now with any question of the wisdom of such regulations. Everyone is agreed that the Government should protect, by all the *practical* means that can be devised, the health of those operatives who work at dangerous processes, or have to handle dangerous substances.

The extent to which State regulations may be carried, depends absolutely on the ability of the manufacturer to carry them into effect without undermining his commercial position.

IV. The Official Statistics of Lead Poisoning.

Statistics may be notoriously made to prove anything. The first thing that the official statistics on lead poisoning prove, is that the pottery industry is responsible for about **one third** only of the total cases provided by the various industries of the country. Moreover the statistics for the three months of 1899, during which the medical examination of certain workers has been brought into force in the pottery industry, prove that while the cases of plumbism during this period, as compared with the same period of 1898, show a large and welcome diminution in the pottery industry, they show a continuous increase in the other trades involved, (see p. 17).

The pottery trade however, has a serious indictment to bring against the way in which the official statistics as to lead poisoning in that industry are presented, and also as to the way in which they are interpreted in the recently issued Home Office Blue Book on "The use of lead compounds in Pottery."

First—Though it is well-known in the trade, and should be equally well-known to the officials who have to deal with it, that the glazes used by various groups of manufacturers contain widely different percentages of lead compounds, and therefore differ as widely in their *toxic intensity*, no distinction is drawn in the returns between the manufacture of china, earthenware, china furniture, sanitary ware, electric fittings, majolica ware, jet and Rockingham wares, which are in many respects quite separate branches of the pottery industry.

Second—There is nothing to show in the returns how many of the reported cases relate to persons attacked for the first time, and how many years such persons have followed their employment.

Third.—There is nothing to show in the returns that a large percentage of the reported cases are those of persons who have already been reported once as suffering from plumbism, but who have been allowed to resume work **by their own medical attendant**, after treatment. It is stated on the authority of Mr. R. Jamieson, Secretary of the Longton and Fenton China Manufacturers' Association, that "out of 404 reported cases, 161 cases or nearly 40 per cent of the whole were repeat cases."

Fourth.—There is nothing to show in the returns whether the cases are slight or serious, or what the proportion of fatal cases is to the total number of reported cases.

Fifth.—When once a case of plumbism has been reported, although subsequent observation may show that the diagnosis of the medical man was incorrect in the first instance, the Home Office refuse to delete such a case from the published totals.

The above considerations show that in attempting to draw any conclusions from statistics compiled as the statistics of lead poisoning are compiled, the greatest care is necessary to avoid sweeping conclusions, which a fuller acquaintance with all the facts might show to be worthless.

We do not propose to deal with the conclusions drawn by writers who cannot know enough about the trade to grasp the significance of the figures, but we will examine the conclusions arrived at by Professors Thorpe and Oliver, on page 9 of their report.

We reprint their tables and the conclusions at which they arrive.

On page 7 of their report they give the following table, which we will designate Table A.

TABLE A.

Number of Persons Employed in Processes where Lead is used in the Manufacture of Earthenware and China.

North Stafford District.—July, 1898.

Persons employed as	Under 13.		13 to 18.		Over 18.	
	Males.	Females	Males	Females	Males	Females
(a) Dippers	—	—	9	15	486	66
(b) Dippers' assistants.	7	—	408	49	103	58
(c) Ware cleaners ...	—	—	15	76	90	382
(d) Glost placers ...	—	—	58	8	1,747	38
(e) Majolica paintresses	—	—	—	62	—	233
(f) Groundlayers ...	—	—	—	9	89	373
(g) Colour dusters ...	—	—	—	24	7	118
(h) Enamel colour and glaze blowers ...	—	—	—	—	9	12
(i) Other persons coming in contact with lead not enumerated in the foregoing list ...	—	—	19	13	76	44
Total	7	—	509	256	2,607	1,324

Males, 3,123; females, 1,580.

Below this they give the total number of cases of reported plumbism during the three years 1896, 1897, and 1898, during which compulsory notification has been in force. They find that this gives the astonishing number of reported cases as 1085 in three years among a stated total of 4703 workers.

Apparently they recognise that this comparison is a most unfair one, and that the only possible plan is to compare the number of cases reported in any one year, with the number of workers employed in one year, as they give on page 9, a table which we will designate Table B.

TABLE B.*

COMPARISON OF NUMBERS OF PERSONS "WORKING IN THE LEAD" IN JULY, 1898, WITH NUMBER OF CASES OF LEAD POISONING REPORTED IN YEAR 1898.

	Workers.		Lead Cases.			
	Males	Females	Males	Per cent	Females	Per cent
Dippers	495	81	41	8·2	7	8·6
Dippers' assistants ...	518	107	20	3·9	19	17·8
Ware cleaners ...	105	458	1	1·0	58	12·7
Glost placers	1,805	46	48	2·6	1	2·0
Majolica paintresses ...	—	295	—	—	31	10·5
Groundlayers	89	382	10	11·3	45	11·8
Colour dusters and litho dusters	16	154	10	62·5	32	20·8
Other persons in contact with lead ...	95	57	22	23·2	3	5·3
Total	3,123	1,580	152	4·9	196	12·4

From Table B they draw the following conclusions:

"It appears from these numbers that of the total male-workers 4·9 per cent. become "leaded" whereas of the female workers the proportion is as high as 12·4 per cent."

*It will be noted that whereas in Table A, the workers are classified according to both age and sex, in Table B they are classified according to sex alone.

On page 11 of the report, in order to support their contention that women and young persons should be excluded from employment as dippers, dippers' assistants, ware cleaners after dippers, and glost placers, after admitting the suitability of the work in other respects they say :—

" There is however no room for doubt that young persons and women between the ages of 17 and 30 are especially susceptible to the influence of lead."

We are aware that this statement represents the opinion of many persons who have practical experience of the influence of plumbous substances on operatives of varying age and sex. But it is directly opposed by the experience of other persons who have for years employed men, women and young persons on works of this class. The evidence of Mr. Regout, given on page 17 of the Home Office report, is a case in point.

We must now see how far the figures given, relating to the whole trade and not to the experience or belief of any particular person, support these two contentions,

(a) that women between the ages of 17 and 30 are more susceptible than men,

(b) that young persons are more susceptible to plumbism than adults.

The fact that of male workers 4·9 per cent. become " leaded " and of female workers 12·4 per cent. seems to prove contention (a) absolutely.

But these figures are worthless for any such purpose as they are arrived at by adding together all the totals, and without any consideration of the fact that the danger is greater in some processes than in others; with some substances than with others; and that the risks are therefore, very unevenly distributed among different classes of workers. Table B shows that 1805, or more than 50 per cent. of the total number of males are employed in the occupation of glost placing, where the proportion of plumbic cases is 2·6 per cent. for the males, and only 2 per cent for the females employed. On the other hand 295 females and not a single male, are employed in Majolica painting, an occupation so dangerous that it induces plumbism in 10·5 per cent. of its workers. As a matter of fact

there is not a single occupation among those specified in Table
B as dangerous occupations, in which male and female workers are
employed in anything like equal proportions. For convenience, we
may prepare another Table, C. giving the numbers only, with the
approximate per centage of men and women employed in each
occupation.

TABLE C.

	Total No. of workers employed	Per-centage of Males employed	Per-centage of Females employed	No. of Males employed	No. of Females employed
Dippers	576	86	14	495	81
Dippers' assistants... ...	625	84	16	518	107
Ware cleaners	563	18	82	105	458
Glost placers	1,851	97·5	2·5	1,805	46
Majolica paintresses ...	295	—	100	—	295
Groundlayers	471	19	81	89	382
Colour dusters and Litho dusters	170	11	89	16	154
Other persons in contact with lead...	152	62	38	95	. 57
Total	4,703	—	—	3,123	1,580

The results arrived at by Professors Thorpe and Oliver are therefore vitiated by the fact that they are obtained by grouping together
irregular proportions of males and females, employed in a number of
occupations which notoriously vary in their toxic power. We have,
for instance, the occupation of glost placing, which is far and away
the least dangerous of all the occupations, and in which the 1851
operatives employed are divided in the proportion of 97·5 per cent.
of males to 2·5 per cent. of females. On the other hand we
have groups like Majolica painting, groundlaying, colour dusting,

in which trades over 80 per cent. of the persons employed are women, and in which the proportion of workers affected by lead ranges from 10·5 per cent. to 20·8 per cent. of those employed.

The utmost that can be made of the figures as they stand is that a certain number of males and a certain number of females are employed in the "Potteries" district of Staffordshire as dippers, dippers' assistants, &c., &c., of whom a certain percentage suffer from plumbism. The Staffordshire "Potteries" however comprises works producing almost every variety of lead-glazed wares known, and we are given no information as to the class of works furnishing the cases. A certain number of the persons in question are employed in china factories, where the glazes generally speaking may contain from 10 to 15 per cent. of lead oxide; a further number are employed in the factories producing earthenware, sanitary ware, electric fittings, &c., where the glazes may contain proportions of lead oxide, varying from 13 to 22 per cent., according to the body used; a third group are employed in the production of Majolica or jet and Rockingham goods, some of the glazes for which contain from 25 to 50 per cent. of lead oxide. It is impossible to deny the validity and force of the above considerations, which prove that the figures given are worthless in so far as they cast any light on the important question of the relative susceptibility of males and females to the influences of plumbism in pottery works. We can only see one way in which such a statement could be irrefutably proved or disproved, viz: by the employment of a given number of male workers and of female workers, who were known to be free from certain hereditary taints, in the same class of work, and on the same materials.

Perhaps the Home Office has such information in its possession?

We have now to deal with the further statement that young persons i.e., those under 18 years of age, are more susceptible than adults. We express no opinion as to the correctness or incorrectness of this statement, we are only concerned to discover how far it is supported by the figures given in the report of Professors Thorpe and Oliver.

To put the matter clearly, we have prepared the following table in which we have placed by the side of the official figures in the table on page 7 of their report, giving the classification of persons employed, the figures given on page 8 of the reported cases of plumbism in the same year.

TABLE D.*

| | Under 18. | | | | | | Over 18. | | | | | |
| | Males. | | | Females. | | | Males. | | | Females. | | |
	Total No. employed.	No. Plumbic cases	Per Cent.	Total No. employed.	No. Plumbic cases	Per Cent.	Total No. employed.	No. Plumbic cases	Per Cent.	Total No. employed.	No. Plumbic cases	Per Cent.
Dippers	9	—	—	15	1	6·6	486	41	8·4	66	6	9·09
Dippers' Assistants ..	415	14	3·4	49	2	4·0	103	6	5·8	58	17	29·3
Ware Cleaners	15	—	—	76	3	3·9	90	1	1·1	382	55	14·2
Glost Placers	58	—	—	8	—	—	1747	48	2·7	38	1	2·6
Majolica Paintresses ..	—	—	—	62	4	6·4	—	—	—	233	27	11·5
Groundlayers ..	—	—	—	9	—	—	89	10	11·2	373	45	12·0
Colour Dusters	—	—	—	24	6	25·0	7	—	—	118	9	8·6
All other Processes ..	19	4	21·0	13	8	61·0	85	28	33·0	56	12	21·0
Total	516	18	3·5	256	24	9·4	2607	134	5·1	1324	172	13·0

So that in the gross, and collecting together workers of similar sex we get:

MALES.

Under 18 } 516 employed, with a percentage of 3·5 of plumbic cases.

Over 18 } 2607 employed, with a percentage of 5·1 of plumbic cases.

FEMALES.

Under 18 } 256 employed, with a percentage of 9·4 of plumbic cases.

Over 18 } 1324 employed, with a percentage of 13·0 of plumbic cases.

*This table was prepared in the first instance by Mr. H. Watkin, (MacIntyre & Co) Burslem.

It may, of course, be pointed out that drawing the line at 18 years of age does not state the case fairly. The line was drawn not by us, but by the Home Office, and endorsed by their experts in the statement that young persons are especially susceptible to the influence of lead.

We can only trust that the next time statistics are quoted officially a little more care may be bestowed on their interpretation, before assuming that they support either one side or the other, of such a vexed question as that of the employment of young persons and women in dipping houses, ware cleaning and glost placing rooms. We may briefly sum up this chapter under the following heads:—

1. About one person in three of those who suffer from plumbism in the Kingdom, does so from following certain employments connected with the manufacture of pottery.

2. The new rules of monthly medical examination, which came into force at the latter end of last year, coupled with the power of suspension from such employment, given to the medical men, have produced in the three first months of this year a striking diminution in the number of reported cases from the pottery industry. (See table p. 17).

3. There has been no corresponding diminution in the number of cases furnished by other trades—on the contrary these cases have increased in number. (See table p. 17).

4. The Official Statistics of Plumbism are presented in such a form that they are almost useless for any just purposes of deduction or comparison.

5. The statements made by Profs. Thorpe and Oliver in their report "On the use of lead in pottery," that young persons, and women between the ages of 17 and 30 are particularly susceptible to the influence of lead, are not proven and are not provable by the official tables given in the report.

6. From the official figures given relating to "The Potteries" district of Staffordshire, it is shown that there are fewer reported cases of Plumbism in young persons, *i.e.*, those under 18 years of age, than in adults ; and the same is true of persons of either sex.

We simply deal in this chapter with the official statistics just as we should deal with any other scientific data. However imperfect in their form such statistics may be, the fact remains, that a serious amount of plumbism exists among certain specified groups of pottery ·workers. When we have allowed all the cases that can be fairly claimed, there will still remain the vital question, as to what proportion of these cases is due to the neglect of the most elementary precautions by the workers themselves. We have now to approach the serious problems involved in grappling with the admitted evils, by methods other than those already in force.

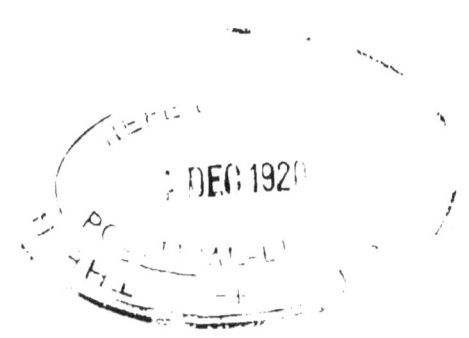

V. The Report of Professors Thorpe and Oliver.

This document, forming the recently issued Blue Book on the use of lead compounds in pottery, is in some respects the most important document that has ever appeared dealing with our trade. During the agitation of last year, the Home Office, probably feeling that it did not possess such knowledge as would enable it to deal adequately with the evils of plumbism, connected with the pottery industry, invited the assistance of two scientific professors, of European reputation, Dr. T. E. Thorpe, F.R.S., Head of the Government Laboratories, and Dr. Thomas Oliver, a physician whose work on lead poisoning forms the most important English contribution to our knowledge on this subject.

They were asked to investigate the problem in the following terms:—

The Secretary of State desires to ascertain

(First) How far the danger may be diminished or removed by substituting for the carbonate of lead ordinarily used either,
(a) One or other less soluble compound of lead ; e.g., a silicate,
(b) Leadless glaze.

(Second) How far any substitutes found to be harmless or less dangerous than the carbonate lend themselves to the varied practical requirements of the manufacturer.

(Third) What other preventive measures can be adopted.

The Blue Book sets forth in simple, direct, and decided terms what the Professors have done, and the conclusions at which they have arrived. Their conclusions are embodied in the four following recommendations :—

1. That by far the greater amount of earthenware, of the class already specified, can be glazed without the use of lead in any form. It has been demonstrated, without the slightest doubt, that the ware so made is in no respects inferior to that coated with lead-glaze. There seems no reason, therefore, why in the manufacture of this class of goods the operatives should still continue to be exposed to the evils which the use of lead-glaze entails.

2. There are, however, certain branches of the pottery industry in which it would be more difficult to dispense with the use of lead compounds. But there is no reason why, in these cases, the lead so employed should not be in the form of a fritted double silicate. Such a compound, if properly made, is but slightly attacked by even strong hydrochloric, acetic, or lactic acid. There can be little doubt that, if lead must be used, the employment of such a compound silicate—if its use could be ensured—would greatly diminish the evil of lead-poisoning.

3. The use of raw lead as an ingredient of glazing materials, or as an ingredient of colours which have to be subsequently fired, should be absolutely prohibited.

4. As it would be very difficult to ensure that an innocuous lead-glaze shall be employed, we are of opinion that young persons and women should be excluded from employment as dippers, dippers' assistants, ware-cleaners after dippers, and glost-placers in factories where lead-glaze is used, and that the adult male dippers, dippers' assistants, ware-cleaners, and glost-placers should be subjected to systematic medical inspection.

Had the Professors chosen to state their conclusions, without at the same time setting forth the ascertained facts and experiments on which those conclusions were based, we should doubtless have been told that after an exhaustive enquiry, on the lines laid down by the Home Secretary, the Professors had arrived at certain conclusions, which the Home Secretary was compelled to accept without listening to anything the potters had to say on their own behalf. Fortunately, however, this course has not been taken, and the Professors have willingly set forth for us the main facts that they have gathered, either from the experience of manufacturers in this country and on the Continent, or from special experiments performed in the Government Laboratories during the course of the investigation. We are, therefore, entitled to examine the conclusions, along with the evidence on which they are based; and if we can show that the evidence contained in the Blue Book is insufficient to support their most drastic recommendations, while other conclusions, better adapted to the manufacturing and commercial conditions of the English pottery trade, would meet all reasonable requirements, we believe that we shall do both the Pottery Industry and the State a real service. We will take the conclusions in the order in which they appear on page 15 of the Report.

The first conclusion is that "by far the greater amount of earthenware, of the class already specified,* can be glazed without the use of lead in any form."

When we turn to the Report for the information on which this very decided statement is based, (See Report, page 9), we find—

"On the occasion of our visit to the Potteries, in June last, we were shown the results of various experiments made in order to obviate the use of lead in glazes, but only in a few cases were the results satisfactory."

"The six months which have elapsed since this enquiry was instituted by the Home Office have witnessed many successful attempts on the part of the manufacturers to substitute leadless glazes for those hitherto in general use."

"*We have no doubt whatever that leadless glazes of sufficient brilliancy, covering power, and durability, and adapted to all kinds of table, domestic, and sanitary ware, are now within the reach of the manufacturer.*"

"We have reason to believe that this fact is now more generally admitted by the trade than it was six months ago."

We will pass by the question as to how far the fact, that one or a dozen manufacturers in Staffordshire have succeeded in glazing **some** of their earthenware with a leadless glaze, proves that leadless glazes are now within the reach of the manufacturer at large.

The statements given above show that the Professors rely on the experience of certain manufacturers during the six months that had elapsed between the commencement of this enquiry and the drafting of the Report to establish their contention. There is, however, a much greater body of practical experience to appeal to than this. It is known, to everyone who has studied the historical development of English Pottery, that many potters of repute, from the great Josiah Wedgwood and his contemporaries to the men of the present day,

---

*On page 12, paragraph 8, they state that this means seven-tenths of the total amount produced by the Staffordshire "potteries."

have made numberless trials and experiments to produce leadless glazes capable of meeting the requirements of our trade. These experiments have been repeated and extended on the Continent, not merely by rule of thumb potters, as we are sometimes contemptuously termed, but by such expert chemists as the late Dr. Seger, at one time head of the Charlottenburg Porcelain Works, who devoted years of experiment to this very point. The only result that has hitherto attended these experiments, conducted in many cases on a very large scale, and in some cases with years of patient trial, has been, generally, **the abandonment of the leadless glaze and a return to glazes containing lead.**

The history of some of these experiments is instructive. In 1820, the Society of Arts awarded a gold medal to Mr. John Rose, of Coalport, Salop, for the discovery of a leadless glaze. This medal had been regularly offered for twenty-five years before that date without producing a single satisfactory glaze. The original offer related to a glaze for earthenware, but the glaze in question was only for china, and hence the award was shorn of a considerable part of its value, as the manufacture of china is on a much smaller scale than the manufacture of earthenware. The composition of this glaze was published far and wide, but as no details were given of the body on which it was placed, and the firing temperature and conditions needful, it never came into extensive use, as it was found, by most potters who gave it a trial, to be quite unsuited to their body or the conditions of firing in use at their works.

In 1865 the subject was brought before the British Association, meeting at Birmingham, by Mr. H. Coghill, of Newcastle-under-Lyme, and a formula was given which was persistently tried by several manufacturers, but with unsatisfactory results. The behaviour of this leadless glaze under varying conditions of firing was so uncertain, and the consequent loss so heavy, that every maker finally abandoned it in favour of leaded glaze. The reader who is anxious for further information as to the experiments that have been undertaken by pottery manufacturers in this direction will find considerable information in a paper on " Leadless Glazes," read before the Society of Arts, by Mr. W. P. Rix, and published in the Society of Arts' Journal of March 3, 1899.

Within the last few months, as the Report states, many manufacturers have made renewed experiments with leadless glazes, but,
as they have nothing to try but what has been tried before, and as the
composition of their glazes (See Report, page 40) shows that they
are very similar to glazes that have been previously tried and found
wanting, one hardly dare hope for any better result than we have had
in the past.

Bearing these facts in mind, and remembering that in this respect
the English potter is in exactly the same position, neither better nor
worse, than his European or American rivals, it is certainly surprising, to say the least of it, to find men of undoubted scientific eminence drawing such a sweeping conclusion from premises so incom-
plete and insufficient.

Further, the Professors have apparently overlooked the fact that
the composition of a glaze is only one factor in the production of
pottery on the commercial scale. We may be told that recent experiments have been conducted on a commercial scale successfully,
but six months is after all too short a period of time to establish beyond doubt a change of such importance, had the results been
obtained by every potter in the country even ; but the fact that a few
firms possess formulæ which have for a period of six months or so
answered their requirements, on a limited portion of their production,
is of very little value to the rest of the trade. except, possibly, as a
starting point for further experiments on their own account. Beyond
all this, there is still the fact, known to every practical potter of repute, and to none better than to those who are trying these glazes at
the present time, that leadless glazes of sufficient stability, *i.e.*, containing a sufficient percentage of alumina to bring them into agreement with the ware, do not fuse in the same way that lead glazes do,
and are absolutely deficient in that covering power, as a potter understands the term, that Professors Thorpe and Oliver claim for them.

At the general firing temperature of white earthenware glazes, a
leadless glaze, even of the very latest type, becomes clear and glossy,
but it does not become fluid. As a potter would say, "There is no
flow in it." It follows from this, that the slightest inequality of thick-
ness produced in the dipping remains after firing ; that any small bit

chipped or knocked out of the glaze coating before it is fired (an accident of the most common occurrence), leaves a bare spot, for the glaze cannot flow over the space in the same way as a lead glaze would; moreover, the mending of imperfectly glazed pieces before firing is rendered impossible for the same reasons. These points, small as they may seem, are of the utmost importance in practical working, for although much greater care must be taken in sorting the biscuit ware before dipping, as well as in the operations of dipping and placing, the proportion of defective pieces may still be altogether too great to be borne.

Another important circumstance adversely affecting the use of leadless glazes from the manufacturer's point of view, and connected with the foregoing, is the fact that in working on the large scale it is not possible to bring the temperature of the firing chamber or oven, (which is generally a cylindrical chamber from 14 to 18 feet in diameter, and from 16 to 20 feet high), to one regular and even temperature. Assuming that in the larger portion of that space the heat is constant and normal, there will still remain portions, amounting to a considerable area in the aggregate, in which it is inconstant and abnormal. These are the ordinary conditions of manufacture, and the potter must possess such glazes as will meet these conditions and still produce a high percentage of best quality goods. Tried by this standard, leadless glazes compare very unfavourably with leaded glazes, as the limits of temperature and firing conditions within which they will produce satisfactory goods are much more restricted than is the case with leaded glazes.

We cannot put the case better than by quoting the words of Dr. Seger, one of the most accomplished chemists ever connected with the pottery industry. He says:—*" Lead oxide is unquestionably the metallic oxide which is best suited for introduction into a glaze. Its insolubility in water, which allows of its employment in the free state, the easy decomposition of its compounds, (e.g., the carbonate and the sulphate), its easy fluidity, which permits of ready entrance into compounds, the low fusibility of its silicates, the many sidedness of the several proportions in which it may be introduced into glazes, almost always giving clear and brilliant glazes; these, together with the high refractivity, as well as the beauty of the coloured lead glazes, are properties which no other metallic oxide possesses."

"And, further, I might here also call attention to the fact that wares covered with a leadless glaze assume on that account a different character. They lose the peculiar brilliancy possessed by lead glazes, and assume more the character of a *porcelain glaze."

"In making the attempt to produce glazes free from lead, I do not mean to pretend that lead can be replaced in all instances. Lead glazes cannot be dispensed with for all those branches of the industry which require an artistic treatment, and endowment of the pottery."

We think these words of the chemist and potter, whose researches on leadless glazes are classical, give point to our contention that Professors Thorpe and Oliver, in making the statement they have done on this matter, have, in their eagerness to solve this troublesome question, not paid sufficient attention to the work previously done on this very point, and have altogether over-estimated the present value of leadless glazes to the trade at large.

Knowing, as we do, that every leadless glaze yet invented, including those recommended by Professors Thorpe and Oliver, is improved in covering power and general working properties, as well as in brilliance and smoothness of finish by the addition of lead compounds, it is unlikely that any English manufacturer of standing dare risk his reputation by confining himself to leadless glazes for his general earthenware trade.

The suggestion that certain public bodies should give a preference to wares glazed without the use of lead compounds, is worthy of attention, as we see in such a recommendation the means of encouraging manufacturers to persevere with their experiments in this direction. One would like to be informed however, what steps the public bodies in question would take to see that they obtained leadless glaze when they asked for it.

Could leadless glazes be discovered, which were applicable to the conditions of what is known as the general earthenware trade,

---

* The porcelain referred to by Dr. Seger is Hard-paste porcelain, a very different product from English china.

an immense stride would have been taken towards absolutely ridding our industry of the slightest risks of plumbism. Every potter wishes devoutly that it lay in his power to abolish lead compounds from the materials on which he has to rely, but Nature is a stern mistress, for after more than a century of experimenting, the problem still remains for solution, and that solution, despite the dictum of the Professors, is not yet attained.

Passing by, therefore, their first recommendation as being outside the range of " Practical Politics," we come to the second, in which they admit that there are certain branches of the pottery industry in which it would be more difficult to dispense with the use of lead compounds, and they recommend that in all such cases the lead employed should be in the form of a double silicate, and they further say that there can be little doubt that the employment of such a silicate would greatly diminish the evils of lead poisoning. (Report, p. 15.)

We think this conclusion represents the actual facts of the case, and it is one which we would urge every potter to adopt. *We go further than that, and say that the report shows that such a method, wherever it has been adopted, has almost entirely removed the evils in question.* In our opinion, this is the only presently practicable method which can be adopted by potters of every class with prospects of success, both in safeguarding the health of the operatives and in enabling manufacturers to conduct their business on lines known to them. Taking the information collected in the Blue Book and arranging it from this point of view, we find the following facts clearly set forth.

(1). Professor Thorpe gives us the percentage of oxide of lead found in a number of glazes used in the Staffordshire " Potteries" for the glazing of ordinary earthenware. (See Report, page 38.) And he also gives us the percentage of oxide of lead contained in the glazes used at certain Continental factories for glazing similar wares. Collecting the figures together that relate to similar classes of goods, we obtain the following tables :—

ENGLISH. *

Old Hall, Hanley	20·05 p.c. of PbO in dry glaze.	
Booth's, Tunstall	15·50 ,, ,, ,,	
T. & R. Boote, Burslem ...	16·14 ,, ,, ,,	
Barker & Read, Fenton ...	22·17 ,, ,, ,,	
Bishop & Stonier, Hanley ...	13·14 ,, ,, ,,	
Barker & Kent, Fenton ...	21·37 ,, ,, ,,	
T. G. Green & Co., Church Gresley	20·42 ,, ,, ,,	
S. Johnson, Burslem ...	15·38 ,, ,, ,,	
Buller's, Hanley	17·70 ,, ,, ,,	
Brough & Jones, Stoke ...	16·86 ,, ,, ,,	

FOREIGN.

Boch Frères, Belgium	22· 0 p.c. PbO.	
Petrus Regout, Holland	13· 3 ,, ,,	
La Société Céramique ₍	18·97 ,, ,,	
Wijck, Holland ₎	18·15 ,, ,,	
The Aluminia Works, Copenhagen	15· 6 ,, ,,	
Rörstrand Works, Stockholm	14· 0 ,, ,,	
Villeroy & Boch, Dresden	17· 7† ,, ,,	

An examination of these figures of Professor Thorpe's shows that, comparing similar glazes, the percentage of oxide of lead used in this country is the same as on the Continent.

(2). We find further these statements made by Professor Thorpe, which are now brought together in tabular form for convenience.

Boch Frères, La Louvière, Belgium.

Glaze in general use contains 22% of lead oxide.

"I was informed by M. Northomb that no cases of plumbism were known to have occurred at this factory during the last twenty years." (Report, page 17).

La Société Céramique, Wijck, Holland.

Glaze contains from 18% to 19% of lead oxide.

---

* The surprising thing about these figures is the close agreement between the highest, lowest, and mean percentage of the two groups.

† See remark on Villeroy & Boch's glaze on next page.

"The Managing Director informed me that he had only known of one case of dropped wrist in the factory in 25 years." (Report page 18).

The Aluminia Works, Copenhagen.

Glaze contains 15·6% of lead oxide, half of which is fritted, and half added raw.

"Mr. Schou (the Managing Director), assured me that there had not been a single case of plumbism at this works." (Report page 20).

Rörstrand Works, Stockholm.

Present glaze contains 14% of lead oxide. A new glaze is proposed containing 17% of lead oxide.

"Since fritted lead was introduced there has been no case of lead poisoning at this works or at the works at Helsingfors." (Report page 20).

Villeroy and Boch, Dresden.

The glaze is stated in the analytical table to contain 10·2% of lead oxide, but calculating from the formula given below it (Report page 25), the percentage works out to 17·7% of lead oxide, which is a much more probable percentage.

"Not a single case of plumbism during 24 years." (Report page 25).

How are we to account for the fact that in all these Continental works, where the glazes are as richly leaded as in similar English works, plumbism is practically unknown. The only answer is, and it is stated in several places in the report, that in those works it is customary to frit the lead, that is, to convert it from the form of carbonate or oxide into the form of a silicate by fusion with sand, flint, or some other siliceous material. In English works the fritting of the lead has been the exception and not the rule. It seems obvious from these facts, which we collect from the report, that if the fritting of the lead with some of the other ingredients of the glaze were made compulsory on all potters using lead in their glazes at all, the same happy results would follow in this country too.

The Professors might have strengthened their report in this direction by including the experience of certain English firms who have used fritted lead, as they say on page 12 of the Report, "In the manufacture of majolica tiles (in which the proportion of lead oxide is very high), many firms frit the greater proportion of their lead. The majority of the severe and fatal cases of lead poisoning arising from majolica tile making have occurred in works in which "raw" lead continues to be used."

For all classes of pottery referred to by Professors Thorpe and Oliver in the first section of their report, and which they state form about seven-tenths of the total output of the potteries (we presume this means the Potteries district of Staffordshire only?), the report shows that it is possible by using a properly compounded silicate to obviate practically all risk of lead poisoning, without resorting to such a drastic and uncertain change as the prohibition of the use of lead in the glaze.

With regard to the glazes richer in lead than those already men-tioned, there can also be no doubt that the same reasoning must apply. For though no mention is made of the fact in the report, and no analyses are given of the glazes used at these Continental factories in the production of majolica wares and tiles, we know that they are used, and used in very large quantities. If, therefore, there have been no cases of lead poisoning at any of these works since the introduction of fritted lead, it is manifest that, if the Government were to prohibit the use of unfritted lead in all glazes and colours used for pottery purposes in this country, they would strike at the very root of the evil.

The third recommendation made in the Report, viz:—"That the use of raw lead in pottery glazes or colours should be absolutely prohibited," will, we are convinced, meet with the approval of every pottery manufacturer in the country. Time must, however, be given to the trade to accommodate itself to this new state of things; and as certain manufacturers, who have already mastered the technical details connected with the use of fritted lead, (these glazes requiring somewhat different treatment from those in ordinary use), have offered to draw up such information as may help the trade at large to overcome these initial difficulties, there should be little trouble experienced in carrying out this recommendation.

Granting this point, we have now to consider certain suggestions not contained in the conclusions themselves, but given in the body of the report. The first of these relates to the particular form of lead compound which may be introduced. Experimental results are given by Professor Thorpe (see Report, pages 28 and 29), which show that the best known lead silicate, the mono-silicate, is almost as soluble as white lead itself, so that such a substitution would, physiologically, offer little advantage over our present English custom. This silicate is somewhat better than white lead in actual practice, because it is not so powdery and dusty, but in face of its ready solubility in dilute acids, these qualities are not sufficient to warrant the potter in using it. Professor Thorpe then goes on to show how he was led to investigate the solubility of certain other silicates, which contain, in addition to oxide of lead, such bases as alumina and lime. On pages 29 to 33 of the report, he gives some details of experiments in this direction, which finally led to his obtaining a compound boro-silicate, which we may for convenience call Thorpe's silicate, and which he states to be practically insoluble in dilute acids. This silicate contains 22 per cent. of lead oxide, and the results of the Professor's experiments are summed up in this statement; "It seems highly probable that frits of the character described will serve most, if not all, of the manufacturers' purposes, as a form in which the lead may be introduced to make the finished glaze, and that their sparingly soluble nature will render them in great measure harmless, though perhaps not entirely so." (Report, page 37). The question is then how far the means pointed out by Professor Thorpe will meet the requirements of the trade.

Let us consider first the value of what we have called Thorpe's silicate, which is stated in the report to be practically insoluble, and therefore, we may believe, harmless. In the first place the publication of the percentage composition of such a silicate, expressed in terms of silica, oxide of lead, alumina, etc., while quite sufficient for the few trained chemists there are connected with the pottery industry in this country, is not of the slightest use to the average potter. Neither does Professor Thorpe improve matters by stating, on page 11, of his report, that such a compound may be made by fritting an intimate mixture of litharge, flint, felspar, tincal and chalk ; or an intimate mixture of litharge, flint glass, borax, china clay and ground flint, seeing that it is impossible to produce from either of these mixtures the substance named; for the first group would give a frit containing more than the 3·9 per cent. of alkalies in the formula, and the second group contains no substance which would give anything like the 8·3 per cent. of lime required. It may be possible to obtain such a substance in a chemical laboratory, either by fusing together pure chemicals in the requisite proportions, or as Professor Thorpe did, by acting on a known frit and dissolving out of it the excess of some of its constituents. Such conditions do not, however, obtain on a manufactory, where the materials used are only approximately pure (sometimes, not even approximately), and alterations of composition due to the fritting processes in use are absolutely certain. There is no evidence in the report that any compound similar to Professor Thorpe's insoluble silicate has been used by potters. MM. Boch Frères, who furnished Professor Thorpe with the frit from which he first prepared his substance, are not shown to have such a frit in use commercially. The frit stated on page 16 of the report to be employed at their works has a very different composition, and in the grinding, a small proportion of "raw" lead is added to their glaze, for reasons which every *potter* will understand.

Though we rejoice to know that in Thorpe's silicate we have a compound containing 22% of oxide of lead, which is practically insoluble in acids, and must therefore be free from toxic effect, we see two serious difficulties which appear likely to prevent its extensive adoption by potters.

First, because it contains less boracic acid and alkalies, and nearly as high a percentage of silica as potters generally find to suit their requirements. Mr. Robert Ålmström points this out in a letter to Professor Thorpe. (See Report, page 25.) If potters are to use this compound, they possess no simple means of introducing the amount of boracic acid and alkalies required to produce a mixture sufficiently fusible for glazing purposes. If these substances are fritted with the lead they destroy its insolubility, and if they are fritted separately with such proportion of silica, lime, &c., as may be admissible in the glaze, the result would be the production of alkaline or boracic frits so soluble in water as to be useless.

Second.—This silicate cannot possibly form the basis of those glazes such as majolica glazes, or the glazes used for the production of jet and Rockingham wares, which contain more than 22 per cent. of lead oxide. It is apparent, therefore, that potters must prepare for themselves compounds which will suit their individual requirements, and which at the same time shall fulfil the condition of containing the lead in a form possessing little solubility. That is, the lead must be introduced either as a bi-silicate, or as a compound silicate containing oxide of lead, alumina, and lime.

We think in this matter Professor Thorpe has been led astray by his endeavour to produce an absolutely insoluble silicate containing oxide of lead.

We are entitled to ask if the absolute insolubility of the frit in dilute acids is a necessity of the case? So far as the evidence contained in the body of the report goes, it is not. At two of the largest of the Continental works visited, those of Mr. Robt. Almström, at Rörstrand, Stockholm, and MM. Villeroy and Boch, at Dresden, the frit consists essentially of a simple bi-silicate of lead, containing about 65 per cent. of lead oxide and 35 per cent. of silica. We consider it, from the scientific point of view, a grave defect in the report that Prof. Thorpe has apparently made no experiments to determine the solubility of this compound (at all events, he mentions none in the report), which he states is used by these important manufacturers with the most satisfactory results as to its toxic properties.

The practical potter's way of meeting the difficulty is shown by Mr. Robert Almström, whose views, as he is a foreign manufacturer, may carry more weight than those of a mere English potter. In a letter written to Professor Thorpe, and given on page 24 of the report he states : " I have succeeded in getting a glaze that is **nearly insoluble in acids**, except strong nitric acid. My glaze is composed of a frit **A**, containing,

Litharge	..	...	39
Flint	...	...	21
Felspar, (Orthoclase) ...	...	10
Felspar, (Oligoclase) ...	...	10

Fritted together.

and of a frit B, containing,

Borax	... ...	... 150
Flint	...	75
China Clay ...		50
Carbonate of Lime ...	...	50

Fritted together.

and flint, china clay, carbonate of lime, in the following proportions.

Frit A ...	...	... 205
Frit B		... 260
Flint ...	...	... 81
China clay ...		... 34
Carbonate of Lime ...	...	20

that is to say, he prepares a Frit A, containing all the lead and sufficient silica, alumina and lime to reduce it to a comparatively insoluble condition. He also prepares a separate frit B, containing all the borax, (the inclusion of which in frit A would defeat his purpose) together with a sufficient amount of siliceous materials to produce a compound boro-silicate practically insoluble in water.

The complete glaze is then made by grinding together certain proportions of frit A, frit B, and the remaining silica, lime, and china clay.

It will be evident that if this final mixture is nearly insoluble in acids, as stated, then frit A, which contains about 50 per cent. of lead oxide united with alumina, lime, alkalies, and silica, must also be nearly insoluble in acids. Mr Ålmström is further to be commended for keeping his borax in a separate frit, as it is well known that the addition of borax or boracic acid, even in small proportions to a frit containing lead, makes that frit more soluble than it otherwise would be. It seems to us that it is only on these lines that the problem can be effectively and practically solved, and we commend them to our fellow manufacturers as offering the likeliest way out of their difficulties.

Another recommendation in connection with the use of lead compounds in glazes, and dealing with earthenware glazes, is expressed in the following words (Report, page 11):—

"In the interest of the public, as well as that of the worker, we would recommend that the amount of fritted lead in the dipping tub, calculated as lead mon-oxide, should not exceed 12 per cent. of the dried material."

There are two points in connection with this statement that demand attention.

First.—The implication that the health of the public is likely to be affected by the amount of lead contained in the glazes used on the ordinary earthen or china ware produced in this country, for culinary or table purposes. Not a tittle of evidence is given to support any such contention, and, as a matter of fact, it has never yet been shown to our knowledge that any glaze produced in this country, on the wares in question, yields an appreciable amount of lead to the action even of acetic acid. If there is such evidence let it be produced, but it seems unfair to introduce such a suggestion by the method adopted in the Report.

Second.—There is no evidence contained in the Report to warrant the idea that the amount of fritted lead oxide present in the dipping tub, should not exceed 12 per cent. by weight, of the dried material. It is stated that the Professors have seen excellent *examples* of ware, glazed with not more than 12 per cent. of lead oxide. No doubt they are perfectly justified in making such a statement, but it is not thereby proven that a glaze containing 12 per cent. of lead oxide is suitable for all the requirements and all the varied conditions of the general earthenware and china trades in this country. Every manufacturer has his own body mixture, his own methods of firing, and his own glazes; they have been developed by long years of experience, and the manufacturer and his workmen would have to spend very considerable time and effort in accommo-dating themselves to any such altered condition. *Above all the Report entirely fails to show that such a condition is required to protect the health of the workpeople.*

The tables already quoted from the Blue Book (see page 40 of this pamphlet) show that at the various continental factories visited, the percentage of lead oxide in the glazes used on earth-enwares is very similar indeed to the percentage used in this country. In no case do these foreign glazes contain as little as 12 per cent. of lead. The average amount contained is about 17 per cent. Yet, these continental factories are stated to be free from plumbism among the workers. We fail to see, therefore, why any such proposal should be adopted in this country, unless it be seriously contended that the English operative is more susceptible to the influences which make for plumbism, than the German, Belgian, or Swede. If not, why do the Professors propose a standard for English pottery that is obviously unnecessary, and the adoption of which would certainly place the English potter at a disadvantage, as compared with his foreign rival.

We have now to refer to the fourth conclusion set forth by the Professors, which is as follows :—

"As it would be very difficult to insure that an innocuous lead " glaze should be employed, we are of opinion that young persons and "women should be excluded from employment as dippers, dippers' "assistants, ware cleaners after dippers, and glost placers, in "factories where lead glaze is used, and that the adult male dippers, "dippers' assistants, ware cleaners, and glost placers, should be "subjected to systematic medical inspection."

Every manufacturer will concur with the last sentence of that statement, for it is exactly the recommendation which manufacturers have previously made to the Home Office, and no one can doubt the value of periodic medical examination, wherever lead compounds are used, even though they have been reduced to a state of comparative harmlessness. It does not appear, however, that the other portions of this conclusion are supported by the evidence contained in the report :—

First.—As to the difficulty of insuring that an innocuous lead glaze shall be employed.

On page 11 of the report, in suggesting that the use of a limited amount of lead as a double silicate might receive legislative sanction, this statement is made—"And we further recommend that the factory inspectors shall be empowered to take samples from the dipping tubs from time to time, and forward them to the Government laboratory, in order to see that this regulation is complied with."

Now, although we are aware that the Government chemists could

not say from an examination of such glazes that they were perfectly
innocuous to those who worked in them, it would be quite possible
to determine the proportion of lead oxide which they would yield to
definite treatment with dilute acid, and this would give us a reasonable criterion of their relative toxic powers. Such examinations,
conducted by the Government chemists, would be of the utmost
value to the manufacturer in pointing out to him how far he was
working on safe lines, and where his methods or preparations still
stood in need of improvement. We claim, that in this matter, manufacturers have a right to all the assistance that the Home Office can
render them, and we are convinced that there is no manufacturer
who would not gladly try any method of dealing with this question
of the use of lead in glazes that is within practical reach.

Second.—The case as to the exclusion of women and young
children is not sufficiently proven in the report to place its necessity
beyond question. Women and young persons are to be excluded
from employment as dippers, dippers' assistants, ware cleaners, and
glost placers ; while they are still to be allowed to work as majolica
paintresses, ground layers, colour dusters, and litho-transfer makers.
Yet we find from a table on page 8 of the report, that under present
conditions, the occupation of Majolica paintresses, ground layers,
and colour dusters, account for a much larger proportion of the total
number of cases, than do the occupations from which it is now proposed to exclude them, in fact, one of the occupations, that of glost
placers, returns positively the smallest percentage of plumbic cases
of any of the known dangerous processes.

We do not propose, however, that the conditions shall be left as
they have been in the past. We propose that the conditions govern-
ing the use of lead, shall be made similar to those existing in certain
Continental factories, where plumbism is practically done away with.
In these continental factories, women and young persons are employed in the very processes from which it is now proposed they
shall be excluded in this country, and not only so, but they are employed in larger proportions in these occupations than is the case in
this country. The report states (page 16) that MM. Boch Frères,
La Louvière, Belgium, employ 24 female dippers in one factory
alone, and there has been no case of lead poisoning on this factory

in twenty years. In July 1898, only 81 female dippers were employed in the whole of the Staffordshire potteries. The report gives no figures as to the foreign employment of women and young persons in the other processes named, but from the personal experience of many manufacturers who are acquainted with continental works, we are convinced that they are more largely employed in these processes than is the general rule in this country. If such be the case, why should the methods which have rid certain continental factories of the evils of plumbism not be sufficient in our works too?

Summarising this section, we obtain the following information from the report of Professors Thorpe and Oliver:—

(1) English potters, generally speaking, use glazes containing "raw," *i.e.*, "unfritted" white lead. This compound finds its way into the system, and being readily soluble in the gastric juice produces an alarming amount of lead-poisoning.

(2) Women and young persons are stated to be more susceptible to lead-poisoning in this way than adult males. The figures quoted do not support this conclusion.

(3) Leadless glazes are being tried by several manufacturers in this country on a limited scale. The results obtained so far may be described as fairly satisfactory; but that they have been tried on an adequate scale, and under sufficiently varying conditions, there is no evidence to prove.

(4) Certain foreign manufacturers, producing pottery similar to that produced in this country, have abandoned the use of "raw" white lead in their glazes.

(5) The glazes stated in the report to be used by these foreign manufacturers contain as large a percentage of lead monoxide as is contained in the glazes used for similar purposes in this country (Compare p. 40).

(6) The lead compound used in these foreign glazes is either a bisilicate of lead ($PbO.2SiO_2$), or a compound silicate containing as bases oxide of lead, alumina, lime, and alkalies (report, pp. 16-25).

(7) Wherever these compounds have been introduced in place of white lead, lead-poisoning has disappeared (report, see p.p. 17, 18, 20, 25).

(8) The foreign manufacturers above mentioned use "leadless" glazes no more than English potters do.

(9) Women and young persons are employed at these factories as dippers, dippers' assistants, ware cleaners after dippers and glost placers, and yet there are no cases of lead-poisoning.

The statements thus briefly presented are an accurate summary of the information contained, on these points, in the report, and it is evident that they furnish no warrant for the first and fourth conclusions arrived at by Professors Thorpe and Oliver. No one doubts that it would make assurance doubly sure to prohibit the use of lead in the glazes used on seven-tenths of the pottery produced in the "potteries" district of Staffordshire. The report contains very little evidence to show that such a cutting of the Gordonian knot is practicable, while it furnishes ample evidence that so drastic a regulation is not required to abolish " plumbism."

Having given our reasons why the conclusions reached by Professors Thorpe and Oliver can be adopted only very partially in the English pottery trade, it is necessary that we should state, in the clearest and most definite manner, what steps we believe the trade could adopt that would meet the demands made on it, and justly made, that the evils of plumbism should be removed as completely as possible from the industry.

Our conclusions, put briefly, are these :—

First.—The Home Office regulations of 1898, which are now in force in every pottery works in this country, are more complete in their requirements as to ventilation, the removal of dust, and the provision of special clothing and washing conveniences, than the regulations enforced in any other State in the world. They also include a most valuable provision for the monthly medical examination of certain workers, coming in contact with lead compounds, together with the power given to the medical inspector of suspending from such employment persons showing symptoms of plumbism. We suggest that they may be wisely strengthened by an extension of such medical examination to all operatives who come in contact with lead compounds, whatever be their sex or age. A further regulation might with advantage be inserted requiring every such operative to brush the teeth and cleanse the mouth before leaving the works, and before partaking of any food or drink, as we are convinced that the main evil arises from the lead which is taken into the mouth and nostrils.

Second.—We beg the Home Office to insist, with their utmost power, that these regulations shall receive a full and fair trial at the hands of manufacturers and operatives alike.

Third.—We believe the time has come when the use of raw lead in glazes may be prohibited. We only ask that sufficient time be given to those manufacturers, who have had no experience in the use of fritted lead compounds, to carry out experiments for their adoption.

The regulations here suggested, if faithfully carried out by both masters and operatives, with the aid of an increased staff of competent Inspectors, are sufficient to remove the evils which we all deplore. The report of Professors Thorpe and Oliver supports these contentions. While, practical potters must differ from the professors as to the means which should be taken in this matter, the foregoing recommendations would not only reduce the cases of plumbism in the Pottery Industry to a minimum, but they are such as every manufacturer could bring into operation without dislocating his business, and the same cannot be said for the recommendations of Professors Thorpe and Oliver.

Finally, in paragraph 9 of their report, the Professors emphasise an important consideration which has been strangely neglected in the newspaper discussion on this subject.

"It must be clearly understood that so long as lead compounds are employed in pottery manufacture, neither the Special Rules of the Home Office nor the precautionary appliances of the manufacturers, will fully achieve their object if the workpeople themselves will not exercise a reasonable amount of care and common sense in obeying these rules and in using these appliances. If the workers will persist in eating their food with dirty fingers, or in places where lead is used; if they will neglect cleanliness of person and clothing, or allow the colours to drop about; or hold their pencils in the mouth; or rub their eyes with unwashed hands, it becomes impossible to protect them from mischief. If lead were more sharp and sudden in its attack as a poison we should probably hear much less of its evil consequences. It is, however, slow and insidious in its action, and persons may be "leaded" to a grave extent for months or even years until some functional disturbance arises which seems to let loose the latent poison. It cannot be too strongly impressed upon the worker in lead that no amount of familiarity with its use ought to breed contempt for its evil power."

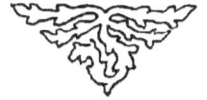

APPENDIX A.

The inclusion of Lead Poisoning under the Provisions of the Workmen's Compensation Act.

Among all the useless and mischievous recommendations for dealing with the evils of plumbism that have been urged in the public press during the agitation on this question, one of the most striking, and oft repeated, was the suggestion that all cases of lead poisoning should be brought under the operation of the Workmen's Compensation Act.

Such a solution of this vexed question is doubtless simplicity itself, when viewed from the editorial chairs of the *London Daily Chronicle* or the *Manchester Guardian*, but there are one or two considerations of elementary justice, which appear to us to destroy this simplicity. In the first place plumbism is hardly in the nature of an accident, seeing that it does not arise from any unusual or accidental occurrence, but from dangers inherent in the ordinary conduct of the business. It would therefore be as reasonable to include lead poisoning under this Act, as say the "Phthisis" of Colliers, or the "Rheumatism" of Agricultural labourers. Secondly, it is always a gradual, and sometimes a lengthy process, frequently taking years to mature. Thirdly, it is almost impossible to say how far the poisoning is due.

(*a*) To constitutional unfitness of the worker.

(*b*) To the careless, reckless, or wilful act of the worker himself.

With reference to the point (*a*), it has long been known that some operatives were much more susceptible to lead poisoning than others, and there is plenty of evidence that certain workpeople are constitutionally prone to contract plumbism. The monthly medical examination is surely the best means of removing such people from callings to which they are unfitted.

With regard to point (*b*), that of the worker's own negligence, Dr. Shadwell, who was sent into the "Potteries" district by the *Times,* states on the authority of Dr. Folker, a medical man of high standing, who has been a factory surgeon in the Hanley district ever since factory surgeons were created, and who speaks therefore from extensive knowledge of the subject, that 17 out of 20 cases of plumbism are caused by carelessness. Mr. Wilson, the Secretary of the Hanley Labour Church, also informed Dr. Shadwell that the apathy of the workpeople was the greatest obstacle the Reform Committee had encountered in their labours on this question.

These considerations are in themselves enough to show how difficult—well nigh impossible—it would be to bring such cases under the clauses of the Workmen's Compensation Act. But there is another question of importance still to be mentioned. In a district like the Potteries district of Staffordshire, where two-thirds of all the people employed in this industry in the kingdom are gathered into a very small area, and where pottery works are consequently in the closest proximity to each other, there is a considerable circulation of workpeople constantly going on from one factory to another. How would it be possible, under such circumstances, to show that the plumbism had been contracted at any particular works? Of course, if the worker had only worked at one place during the whole of his working life, the question, as to where the illness had been contracted might be simple enough. But, speaking from personal experience, we should say that in the majority of cases it is precisely the worker who is careless and indifferent as to his own health, who most frequently changes about from one works to another. Moreover, there are workmen in the Potteries employed in these dangerous occupations who work for various employers, according as each manufacturer has work to be done in his particular branch.

These considerations, which can only be known to those inside the trade, are the very ones which make the inclusion of plumbic cases within the chapter of accidents coming under the Workmen's Compensation Act undesirable, even from the point of view of the operative himself, as in many cases it would be impossible for any judge to be certain as to the liability of any particular employer.

APPENDIX B.

Mr. H. J. Tennant, M.P., and Arbitration in the Pottery Trade.

When a member of Parliament, who is also Chairman of the "Departmental Committee upon Dangerous Trades," states publicly, not only in political speeches, but in a magazine article,* that the power given to manufacturers, under the Act of 1891, to appeal to Arbitration if necessary, against any of the special regulations drawn up by the Home Office for their trade, should be abolished; and that, "The Home Secretary should be empowered to make such regulations as he may consider necessary" the manufacturers referred to must deal with such statements, and endeavour to show how prejudiced and unfair they are.

The assumption underlying these statements is that the Home Office not only knows the principles that must be applied in safeguarding the health of operatives in particular trades, but that its officials know, better than those who carry on the trades, how such principles can be applied in the form of Departmental Regulations. That such an assumption merely begs the whole question, Mr. Tennant is apparently unaware. No such assumption has ever been made by the Home Office itself, and judging by past experience is not likely to be made. The custom of the Home Office has hitherto been to confer with manufacturers, operatives and officials, knowing perfectly well that the men who conduct manufacturing concerns must have a more perfect knowledge of the details of their processes than can be possessed by officials who visit their works only at intervals.

The history of the special regulations that have been proposed by the Home Office for the pottery trade, proves this contention absolutely. Two main sets of regulations have been issued from the Home Office, dealing with this industry. In 1891 the Home Secre-

---

*"Dangerous Trades; a case for Legislation," by H. J. Tennant, M.P.—*Fortnightly Review,* February, 1899.

tary was empowered by Parliament to issue special regulations for certain trades. In November, 1892, Mr. W. Dawkins Cramp, H.M. Superintending Inspector of Factories for the district including North Staffordshire, was asked to report on the pottery works of that district, with special reference to improvements recently introduced by certain manufacturers for dealing with the problems of "dust" and the use of lead compounds. In 1893 Mr. Asquith, the then Home Secretary, appointed a Departmental Committee, consisting of S. W. May, W. D. Cramp, and J. H. Walmsley, (Factory Inspectors), J. T. Arlidge, and W. D. Spanton, (Medical men of eminence, long resident in the "Potteries" district of Staffordshire) and A. P. Laurie (a chemist of repute), to investigate the conditions existing in the "Potteries" district, and to draft special rules. It was apparently not considered necessary by Mr. Asquith to add to this committee anyone possessing a practical knowledge of the industry, either as a manufacturer or as an operative. This is the fundamental mistake that the Home Office has made in all the investigations it has undertaken into one of the most intricate and detailed manufacturing processes known in the world. The report of this Committee of Inquiry contained a draft set of rules which will be found in full (in so far as they relate to the duties of manufacturers) in Appendix C (p. 65). In the body of the report it is stated "that there is less prevalence of plumbism among the pottery population than in past times, and this, notwithstanding the growing number of factories and workers." (See p. 6 of their report.) On page 19 of the same report we find the following remarkable statement:—

" A very long discussion ensued on a proposal 'that a special rule
" should be made requiring manufacturers to arrange for a weekly or
" monthly visit by a doctor, who shall examine *every* worker employed
" in the dangerous processes.' The Committee were divided in
" opinion, the non-official members being in favour, the official mem-
" bers against. The proposal was therefore lost, but is included in
" the recommendations given above."

Why was this most valuable regulation, as well as the one relating to the age of employment, dropped from the subsequent Home

Office rules? Certainly not because of any opposition on the part of manufacturers or operatives.

Acting on this report the special rules, of 1894, were drawn up by the Home Office. These rules could not be accepted by some of the manufacturers as they prescribed certain conditions that could never have been carried out. The Home Secretary, finally sent down into the "Potteries" Mr. G. W. E. Russell, M.P., as a special commissioner, to confer with manufacturers and operatives as to their objections. This meeting was not a resort to arbitration, but was a sensible method of arriving at a *modus vivendi*, which the Home Office might have adopted earlier, with advantage to all concerned.

The main regulation in the draft rules to which manufacturers objected was one fixing the temperature of pottery workshops. The manufacturers contended that the rule, as drafted, was impossible of application. After hearing their arguments, Mr. Russell agreed with them, and on behalf of the Home Office, accepted the amended form, which now appears in rule 6 of the printed regulations of 1894 (see Appendix C., p. 68.)

Will Mr. Tennant contend that his statement in the *Fortnightly Review*, February 1899, page 317, that "objections were raised by the employers, and to save delay and expense of arbitration, certain compromises were arrived at, and the accepted and **attenuated** special rules received the force of law," is a fair and honest description of what actually took place?

After the conference at which Mr. Russell attended on behalf of the Home Secretary, manufacturers pointed out that the rules as drafted contained no provision for the safe custody of the overalls specified in Rule 1, during the week, and suggested an addition, which was of course accepted by the Home Office, that the manufacturers themselves should, in the words of Rule 1, of September 1894, "make arrangements for the safe custody of all overalls and head coverings worn by their operatives."

In the following year a Factories and Workshops Bill was introduced in the House of Commons by Mr. H. H. Asquith, M.P. In April, 1895, while this Bill was before Parliament, a conference was held at Stoke-on-Trent between manufacturers, the local members of Parliament, H.M. Inspector of Factories, and Certifying Surgeons for the district. Dr. Folker brought before this conference the question of periodical medical examination for all workers in lead. This suggestion was warmly supported by the manufacturers, and the local members of Parliament were desired to introduce an amendment to this effect in the measure under discussion.

Before the proposals could, however, be embodied in the measure, the Government was defeated on the Cordite question, and in order that their Factory Bill might be saved, it was treated as a noncontentious measure, and the valuable amendment proposed by the manufacturers was not included in it. No one can blame the Home Office or the Government of the day for this, but the occurrence was a severe misfortune, principally of course to the operatives employed, but also to the manufacturers, who have had to bear the vituperation and abuse showered on them by Mr. H. J. Tennant and others, because, forsooth! it is said that they have suggested nothing, and done nothing for the well-being of those whom they employ.

Mr. Tennant goes on to say, " four years later the breakdown of the rules of 1894 became manifest."

We demur entirely to the truth of any such statement. If breakdown there was, it was due to the failure of the Home Office to see that its special rules were obeyed by manufacturers and operatives. These rules must have added enormously to the work of H.M. Inspector of Factories for the pottery district. The Home Office however made no increase in the staff in this district, and although they have in Mr. J. H. Walmsley an inspector of ability and tact, it was manifestly impossible for one inspector to adequately overlook a district containing some thousands of pottery workshops where trades of greater or less danger are constantly carried on.* So far from there being any breakdown of the rules themselves, they were re-enacted in the rules issued from the Home Office in 1898. The experience gained during the four years of their operation showed that they required strengthening in certain particulars, and that they might be extended to certain other operations, but the only additional rules of serious moment proposed by the Home Office itself in 1898, were Rules 1 and 2. The first of these, Rule 1 of 1898 enacts that after August

---

* An additional sub-inspector has recently been appointed in this district.

1st, 1898, no person under 14 years of age, and after August 1st, 1800, no person under 15 years of age shall be employed in certain specified processes.

With reference to this rule we may point out that the first section of this rule formed the first recommendation of Mr. Asquith's committee of inquiry in 1893. Manufacturers accepted this proposal at the time. The Home Office did not, with the result, that the children of the Potteries, generally speaking, had to wait until 1898 for a regulation which they might have had in 1894.

The second of these new rules, Rule No. 2 of 1898, sets forth that all women and young persons employed in the places and processes named in Rule 1 shall be examined once a month by the certifying surgeon for the district, who shall have power to order suspension from such employment in cases where it is found to be inimical to the health of certain operatives.

This is however the rule debated by Mr. Asquith's committee of inquiry and rejected by the votes of the official members; revived again by the manufacturers themselves in 1895, but not included in the act of that year because of the political exigencies already mentioned. Even in 1898 the Home Office did not include adult males as the manufacturers proposed to do in 1895. Many manufacturers were so convinced of the value of this precaut on that they adopted it *without waiting for the Home Office*.

In every other respect the rules of 1898 differ mainly from the rules of 1894 in wording only, and in the attempt to make certain provisions more definite.

We now come to the point on which Mr. Tennant mainly relies to prove his contention, that the power of resorting to arbitration given by the Act of 1891 to manufacturers, has been so used, to whittle away the value of these regulations, that it ought to be taken away from manufacturers altogether.

Notice of the proposed special rules of 1898 was issued to about 690 manufacturers. Of this number, by far the greater part either took no notice of the rules, or accepted them in the mistaken belief that they would thus quiet the agitation going on in the press. About 100 manufacturers, however, some of whom possess the

best works of their kind in this country, and who had long been in
the habit of doing far more than the Home Office required at their
hands, came to the conclusion that the rules as drafted were incapa-
ble of application in many factories: and as (unlike Mr. H. J.
Tennant) they believed they had sufficient intelligence to understand the principles underlying the Home Office regulations, and
knew the details of their business so thoroughly as to know
what could, and what could not, be carried out in practice, they
proposed certain amendments to the rules.

This was done, not as Mr. Tennant suggests, to emasculate
valuable provisions, *but to express the intentions of the Home Office in
such a way that there could be no dispute as to their practicability*.

In order that the Home Office might have these amendments laid
before it in the clearest possible way, the Encaustic Tile Manufacturers' Association printed in parallel columns, the rules as originally
issued, and the rules as they proposed to amend them, with the
amendations printed in italics. Had the Home Office been prepared
to discuss matters with the dissentient manufacturers in an informal
way, the whole trouble might have been avoided; but the Home
Office, without giving any reasons for its decision, informed these
manufacturers that their amendments could not be accepted; that
Mr. Chester Jones (a barrister) had been appointed to act as Home
Office arbitrator, and that, unless the manufacturers appointed an
arbitrator on their side within twenty-one days, he would proceed
to hear and decide any objections laid before him.

It cannot be said, therefore, that manufacturers sought arbitra-
tration. It was thrust on them by the action of the Home Office.
As manufacturers had put forward their amendments only after the
most careful consideration, and as their proposals related entirely to
questions of practical detail, and did not in the least involve any of
the principles underlying the rules, they felt compelled to abide by
the position they had taken up.

The manufacturers appointed Mr. A. P. Llewellyn, solicitor, as their
arbitrator, and the two arbitrators selected J. S. Dugdale, Esq., Q.C.,
to act as umpire, Mr. Dugdale's being the first name suggested by the

Home Office arbitrator. This procedure was in the form prescribed by the Act of 1891, where it is stated that, in the event of the disagreement of the selected arbitrators, they may appoint an umpire; but if they cannot agree upon a person, the Chairman of Quarter Sessions appoints an umpire. The umpire's decision is final in either case.

Referring to the general question of this method of arbitration, Mr. Tennant, in the article, to which we take exception, uses these words, " Thus matters which ought to be settled by the Secretary of State, with the guidance and control of Parliament, are taken out of his hands and placed either in those of a prejudiced or of an irresponsible power."

As the umpire of the Pottery's arbitration was a well-known public servant of eminent ability and trained judicial capacity we assume that Mr. Tennant will hardly consider his remarks about "prejudiced and irresponsible power" applicable to this particular case—yet they were penned months after the arbitration had taken place and in an article of which it forms the principal theme.

In opening the case for the Home Office, Counsel, on their behalf naturally made the most of the point that the Rules had been adopted, or at all events not objected to, by 607 out of the 691 manufacturers who had received them, but he frankly admitted that the Home Office knew the dissentient manufacturers to be perfectly honest and sincere in the amendments they had proposed.

We quote the words actually used by Mr. Sutton, as taken from the transcribed notes of the Official Shorthand Reporter:—" They " have not made any objection in a vexatious spirit. They have not " availed themselves of any technical difficulty as regards this arbi- " tration. On the contrary, wherever any difficulty has arisen they " have shown a most conciliatory spirit.......I say again as regards " these objections that are before you for discussion in my opinion, " and I say it on behalf of the Secretary of State, they are all worthy " of consideration. I shall not say and I have no instructions to say " a single word which would lead your mind to think that these " gentlemen had taken up an attitude they thought right to take up " from any improper motive whatsoever."

After a patient hearing for two days the net result of the arbitration was that the majority of the amendments proposed by the manufacturers were shown either to the satisfaction of the arbitrators, or of the umpire, to be reasonable and practicable. In fact so much was the umpire impressed by the common-sense reasons on which the manufacturers had based their case, that in concluding the arbitration he said :—" This was a case in which the expense of the arbitration and award ought to be borne by the Treasury, and that he should so recommend."

The Rules as so amended will be found in Appendix C (p. 74), and a perusal of them by any fair-minded person will show, that while the manufacturers never sought to interfere with the principle underlying any of the Rules, they succeeded in impressing upon some of them a practicability which they would otherwise have lacked. It is to this arbitration, however, that Mr. Tennant refers in the Article already quoted when he says:—"If doubt should exist in the mind of anyone as to the inefficiency, nay the absolute mischievousness of the practical application of arbitration, it should be removed by a consideration of the events which have occurred in relation to the Pottery trade."

We would respectfully submit to Mr. Tennant, and to all whose minds are not warped or prejudiced by sensational journalism, that the very opposite is the fact. Whether our view or Mr. Tennant's is the fair and correct one, we confidently leave to the judgment of our readers. This is the only instance in which the power to arbitrate has been used by any considerable body of pottery manufacturers, and this is the case on which Mr. Tennant relies to support his statement that "the abolition of the power of objection is imperative."

Three conditions must be fulfilled by any rules that are proposed for the regulation of an industry:

1st. That the workpeople can understand the object of the rules.

2nd. That the rules are such as manufacturers can apply or enforce.

3rd. That the Factory Inspector can detect infractions of the rules by either master or operatives.

Workers will not obey, neither can masters put into operation rules unsuited to the requirements of any particular factory or business. In face of such a state of affairs (of not infrequent occurrence in the past), what can the Factory Inspector do? He can summon the offenders before the Magistrate, and they may be fined or even imprisoned. But what then? The Factory Inspector cannot live on one particular works, and the law will be evaded or broken. Is it not therefore better, from every point of view, that before rules are issued from the Home Office, those who are responsible for drafting the rules should confer with the manufacturers and operatives' organisations as to the best practical way of giving effect to the principles which the Home Office may desire to enforce? It appears to us that the holding of such a conference before new rules are issued is infinitely preferable to arbitration afterwards.

In any case arbitration is the manufacturers' last resort from the regulations of the well meaning Doctrinaire, like Mr. H. J. Tennant, who would apparently legislate first and ascertain his facts afterwards, and as such, it cannot be abandoned. At a time when arbitration is being put forward as the universal panacea for commercial disputes, the attempts to be-little it made by Mr. Tennant seem woefully out of date.

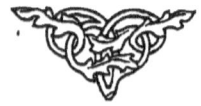

APPENDIX C.

Proposed Special Rules, drafted by Departmental Committee, July, 1893.

The Manufacture of Earthenware and China.

Duties of Occupiers.

1. They shall not allow any child under 14 to be employed in the dipping house or dippers' drying room, or in any processes of ware cleaning after the dipper, glost placing, china scouring, groundlaying, or majolica painting, or in any process in which lead is used.

2. They shall provide suitable overalls and head coverings for all workers employed in the places and processes referred to in Rule 1, and shall have the said articles washed on the premises, and shall also provide a place in which the workers can deposit clothing put off during working hours.

3. They shall not allow any persons (either adult males or others) to cook or partake of any food, or to remain during meal times in the dipping house, dippers' drying room, china scouring room, glost placer's shop, groundlaying shop, or majolica painting room.

4. They shall adopt efficient measures in the processes of towing of earthenware and of the scouring of china for the removal of all dust and flint by fans or other mechanical means; and in all dusty processes they shall adopt measures for dealing with avoidable dust, and for the prevention of any injurious effects arising therefrom, either by the use of mechanical fans or other efficient means.

5. They shall provide brooms, brushes, and all other necessaries for the daily sweeping of floors of workshops, and of such stoves as are entered by the workers, and for the cleansing of work benches and of stairs leading to workshops; and shall arrange that the floors of such workshops and stoves are sprinkled and swept every working

day, and the scraps and dirt removed, and that work benches and stairs are cleansed at least once a week. The daily sweeping of floors of potter's shops shall be done after work has ceased for the day, unless there is some sufficient reason to the contrary.

6. They shall provide washing conveniences with a sufficient supply of water, soap, nail brushes, and towels for all workers employed in the places and processes referred to in Rule 1, and the washing apparatus shall be in convenient proximity to the work places.

7. They shall arrange that the temperature of potters' workshops outside the drying stoves, when people are working there, shall not exceed 80° F., if the outside temperature is below 70° F.; and when the temperature outside is above 70° F., the inside temperature shall not be more than 10° higher.

8. They shall not allow any female under 16 years of age to be employed at treading the lathes used by turners.

Special Rules of 1894, as finally adopted.

The Manufacture of Earthenware and China.

Duties of Occupiers.

1. They shall provide suitable overalls and head coverings for all female workers employed in the dipping house or dippers' drying room, or in any processes of ware cleaning after the dipper, glost placing, china scouring, ground laying or majolica painting (which overalls and head coverings shall remain the property of the employers), and shall make arrangements for the safe custody of all overalls and head coverings worn by their operatives, and for the safe delivery thereof at the works every seven days to the representatives of the laundry or wash house which shall be selected by the operatives for the purpose of washing the same. They shall also provide a place in which the above workers can deposit clothing put off during working hours.

2. They shall not allow any persons to cook or partake of any food, or to remain during meal times in the dipping house, dippers' drying room, china scouring room, glost placers' shop, ground laying shop, or majolica painting room.

3. In the process of towing of earthenware, they shall use fans or other mechanical means for the removal of all dust; in the process of scouring china, they shall, as far as practicable, use mechanical or other efficient means for the removal of flint; and, in all processes and descriptions of manual labour, they shall, as far as practicable, adopt measures for the removal of dust, and for the prevention of any injurious effects arising therefrom, either by the use of mechanical fans, ventilation, or other efficient means.

4. They shall provide brooms, brushes, and all other necessaries for the daily sweeping of floors of workshops, and of such stoves as

are entered by the workers; and for the cleansing of work benches, and of stairs leading to workshops; and shall arrange that the floors of such workshops and stoves are sprinkled and swept every working day, and the scraps and dirt removed, and that work benches and stairs are cleansed at least once a week. The daily sweeping of floors of potters' shops shall be done after work has ceased for the day, unless there is some sufficient reason to the contrary.

5. They shall provide washing conveniences and a sufficient supply of water, soap and nail brushes for all workers employed in the dipping house or dippers' drying room, or in any processes of ware cleaning after the dipper, glost placing, china scouring, ground laying, or majolica painting, as close as is practicable to the workshops.

6. All stoves, as well as all workshops and all parts of the factories, shall be effectually ventilated. Regard being had to the cubic capacity of the shops, etc., there shall be, wherever practicable, natural ventilation by doors and windows; and careful supervision of hot air and hot water pipes used for heating, and of the consumption of gas. The required ventilation shall be accomplished by mechanical or other efficient means. The temperature of any workshop during working hours shall not be allowed to exceed 90 degrees (Fahrenheit).

Rules Proposed by Home Office in 1898.[*]

Duties of Occupiers.

Age.

1. After August 1st, 1898, no person under 14 years of age, and after August 1st, 1899, no person under 15 years of age, shall be employed in the

Dipping house, or | Dippers' drying room,
or in any processes of—

Ware cleaning after the dipper, | Majolica painting,
Glost placing, | Glaze blowing,
Colour dusting, | Transfer making,
Ground laying, | or
 | China scouring.

Monthly Examination.

2. All women and young persons employed in the places and processes named in Rule 1 shall be examined once a month by the Certifying Surgeon for the District, who shall after August 1st, 1898, have power to order suspension from employment in any place or process named in Rule 1.

No person after such suspension shall be allowed to work in any of the places or processes named in Rule 1 without the written sanction of the Certifying Surgeon.

Health Register.

3. A register, in the form which has been prescribed by the Secretary of State for use in earthenware and china works, shall be kept, and in it the Certifying Surgeon will enter the dates and results of his visits, the number of persons examined, and particulars of any directions given by him. This register shall contain a list of all persons employed in the places and processes named in Rule 1, and shall be produced at any time when required by H.M. Inspector of Factories or by the Certifying Surgeon.

---

*These rules were accepted by the occupiers of, and are now in force at, about 470 factories.

Overalls and head coverings.
4. The occupier shall provide and maintain suitable overalls and head coverings for all women and young persons employed in the places and processes named in Rule 1.

All overalls and head coverings shall be kept in proper custody, and all overalls shall be washed at least once a week, and suitable arrangements shall be made for carrying out these requirements.

A suitable place shall be provided in which the above workers can deposit clothing put off during working hours.

Food.
5. No person shall be allowed to prepare or partake of any food or drink, or to remain during mealtimes, in the dipping house or dippers' drying room or in a place in which is carried on any process named in Rule 1.

The occupier shall make suitable provision to the reasonable satisfaction of the Inspector in charge of the district for the accommodation during mealtimes of persons employed in such places or processes.

Dust.
6. After January 1st, 1899, the process of—

Towing of earthenware, Colour dusting,
China scouring, Glaze blowing, or
Ground laying, Transfer making

shall not be carried on without the use of exhaust fans for the effectual removal of dust.

In the process of ware cleaning after the dipper, exhaust fans shall be used, or arrangements made for the dust to fall into water.

In all processes the occupiers shall, as far as practicable, adopt efficient measures for the removal of dust and for the prevention of any injurious effects arising therefrom.

Ventilation.

7. All drying stoves as well as all workshops and all parts of factories shall be effectually ventilated to the reasonable satisfaction of the Inspector in charge of the district.

Lavatories.

8.—The occupier shall provide and maintain sufficient and suitable washing conveniences for all persons employed in the places and processes named in Rule 1, as near as is practicable to the places in which such persons are employed.

The washing conveniences shall comprise soap, nail-brushes, and towels, and at least one lavatory basin for every five persons employed as above, and each such basin shall be fitted with waste-pipe, and have a constant supply of water laid on by tap.

Cleansing of work-places.

9. The occupier shall see that the requirements of Rule 16 are duly observed, and shall provide brushes and all other necessaries for the purpose.

Boards.

10. The boards used in the dipping-house, dippers' drying-room or glost placing shop shall be cleansed every week, and shall not be used in any other department.

Duties of Persons Employed.

Monthly Examination.

11. All women and young persons employed in the places and processes named in Rule 1 shall present themselves at the appointed time for examination by the Certifying Surgeon as provided in Rule 2.

No person after suspension by the Certifying Surgeon shall work in any of the places or processes named in Rule 1 without the written sanction of the Certifying Surgeon.

Overalls.

12. Every person employed in the places and processes named in Rule 1 shall, when at work, wear an overall suit and head covering, which shall not be worn outside the factory or workshop, and which shall not be removed therefrom except for the purpose of being washed.

The overalls and head coverings, when not being worn, shall be deposited in the place provided for the purpose under Rule 4.

Clothing put off during working hours shall be deposited in the place provided for the purpose under Rule 4.

Food.

13. No person shall remain during meal-times in the dipping house, dippers' drying room, or in any place in which is carried on any process named in Rule 1; or prepare or partake of any food or drink therein at any time.

Ventilation.
Dust.

14. No person shall in any way interfere, without the knowledge and concurrence of the occupier or manager, with the means and appliances provided by the employers for the ventilation of the workshops and stoves and for the removal of dust.

Washing.

15. No person employed in any place or process named in Rule 1 shall leave the works or partake of meals without previously and carefully cleaning and washing his or her hands.

Cleansing of work-places.

16. The persons employed shall be responsible for the daily sprinkling and sweeping of the floors of workshops and of such stoves as are entered by the workpeople; and for the daily removal of dust, scraps, ashes, and dirt; and for the weekly cleansing of workbenches and of stairs leading to workshops.

Each person shall be responsible for the cleansing of that portion of the room in which he or she is employed.

Cleansing of work-places.— continued. The sweeping of the floors of potters' shops, stoves, dipping houses, and majolica painting rooms shall be done after working hours by an adult male, employed and paid by the workers and approved by the employer.

Boards. 17. The boards used in the dipping house, dippers' drying room, or glost placing shop shall be cleansed every week, and shall not be used in any other department.

Special Rules as finally settled by Arbitration, 1898.*

Duties of Occupiers.

Age.

1. After August 1st, 1898, no person under 14 years of age, and after August 1st, 1899, no person under 15 years of age, shall be employed in the

| Dipping house, or | Dippers' drying room, |

or in any processes of—

Ware cleaning after the dipper,	Majolica painting,
Glost placing,	Glaze blowing,
Colour dusting,	Transfer making,
Ground laying,	or
	China scouring.

Monthly Examination.

2. All women and young persons employed in the places and processes named in Rule 1 shall be examined once a month by the Certifying Surgeon for the District, who shall, after August 1st, 1898, have power to order suspension from employment in any place or process named in Rule 1. No person, after such suspension, shall be allowed to work in any of the places or processes named in Rule 1 without the written sanction of the Certifying Surgeon.

Health Register.

3. A register, in the form which has been prescribed by the Secretary of State for use in earthenware and china works, shall be kept, and in it the Certifying Surgeon will enter the dates and results of his visits, the number of persons examined, and particulars of any directions given by him. This register shall contain a list of all persons employed in the places and processes named in Rule 1, and shall be produced at any time when required by H.M. Inspector of Factories or by the Certifying Surgeon.

---

* These rules are in force in about 100 factories.

Overalls and Head coverings. 4. The occupier shall provide and maintain suitable overalls and head coverings for all women and young persons employed in the places and processes named in Rule 1.

All overalls and head coverings shall be kept by the occupier in proper custody, and shall be washed at least once a week, and suitable arrangements shall be made for carrying out these requirements.

A suitable place shall be provided in which the above workers can deposit clothing put off during working hours.

Food. 5. No person shall be allowed to prepare or partake of any food or drink, or to remain during meal times in the dipping house or dippers' drying room, or in a place in which is carried on any process named in Rule 1.

The occupier shall make suitable provision to the reasonable satisfaction of the Inspector in charge of the District for the accommodation during meal times of persons employed in such places or processes, with a right of appeal to the Chief Inspector of Factories. Such accommodation to be provided in any room or rooms on the premises other than those referred to in Rule 1.

Dust. 6. After January 1st, 1899, the process of:—

Towing of earthenware	Colour dusting
China scouring	Glaze blowing, or
Ground Laying	Transfer making

shall not be carried on without the use of exhaust fans for the effectual removal of dust, or other efficient means for the effectual removal of dust, to be approved in each particular case by the Secretary of State, and under such conditions as he may from time to time prescribe.

**Dust.
continued.**

In the process of ware cleaning after the dipper, exhaust fans shall be used, or arrangements made for the dust to fall into water.

In all processes the occupiers shall, as far as practicable, adopt efficient measures for the removal of dust and for the prevention of any injurious effects arising therefrom.

Ventilation.

7. All drying stoves as well as all workshops and all parts of factories shall be effectually ventilated to the reasonable satisfaction of the Inspector in charge of the district.

Lavatories.

8. The occupier shall provide and maintain sufficient and suitable washing conveniences for all persons employed in the places and processes named in Rule 1, as near as is practicable to the places in which such persons are employed.

The washing conveniences shall comprise soap, nail brushes and towels, and at least one wash-hand basin for every five persons emp oyed as above, with a constant supply of water laid on, with one tap at least for every two basins, and conveniences for emptying the same and running off the waste water on the spot down a waste pipe.

Cleansing of work places.

9. The occupier shall see that the requirements of Rule 16 are duly observed, and shall provide brushes and all other necessaries for the purpose.

Boards.

10. The boards used in the dipping house, dippers' drying room or glost placing shop, shall be cleansed every week, and shall not be used in any other department, except after being cleansed.

Regulations in Force in Foreign Countries.*

In addition to the regulations in force in Holland, quoted by Professor Thorpe (Blue Book, p. 18), the Home Office has received, through the Foreign Office and from other sources, the following information as to the action that has been taken in foreign countries for protecting the workpeople from lead poisoning in the manufacture of china, earthenware, and porcelain.

France.

The attention of the Minister of Commerce and Industry has been repeatedly called to the effects of lead poisoning in potteries. The suggestion was made that the employment of women, female young persons, and children under 18 years of age, should be prohibited, but it was thought that the risks of poisoning could be obviated by the strict observance of Article 6 of the Decree of 10th March, 1894 :—

"Dust, as well as noxious, unwholesome, or poisonous gases, shall be drawn straight out of the workroom the instant they are produced. To deal with fumes, gases, or light dust, hoods with exhaust chimneys, or any other equally good method of extraction, shall be put up. In the case of dust arising from millstones, beating apparatus, crushers, and all other machines worked by power, drums shall be erected round such machines connected with a system of powerful fans. In the case of heavy gases, such as mercurial or carbon disulphide fumes, a down draught shall be used. The work tables or machines shall be in direct connection with the fan. The work of crushing, sifting, and packing irritating or poisonous material shall be done in closed vessels. The air of the workrooms shall be renewed from time to time, so that it remains in such a state of purity as is necessary for the health of the workpeople."

---

* These regulations are reprinted verbatim from the report of Professors Thorpe and Oliver, pp. 46-50.

Germany.

The Imperial Government have not made special regulations for the manufacture of earthenware and china.

The following is an Order of the President of Police in Berlin relating to the prevention of lead poisoning in potteries, dated January 22, 1888 :—

1.—So-called "fritted" glazes only shall be used in which the lead oxide is united with silicic acid, constituting with this a lead silicate.

2.—Furnaces and ovens in which the fritting is carried on shall be so arranged that the lead fumes developed in the process shall not penetrate into the workroom, but shall either be carried with the products of combustion up the chimney, or be conveyed into a flue directly connected with the furnace.

3.—In order to avoid dust, lead glazes shall only be ground when moistened.

4.—All persons employed in crushing, sieving, and mixing lead glazes, or in sweeping up the glaze when dried, shall wear a sponge over their nose and mouth. This sponge shall, at least three times a day, be washed in clean water mixed with half its bulk of vinegar, and it must always be kept clean. For carrying out this regulation the occupier shall also be responsible.

5. The rooms in which the glaze is made, and those in which the dried glaze requires to be swept up, shall be so situated and ventilated that abundance of fresh air can enter and foul air be removed. Cellar rooms are unsuitable.

6. The occupier shall provide suitable washing conveniences and soap, and facilities for washing out the mouth and cleaning the teeth, as well as for cleaning the clothes.

7. No food or drink (not even water) shall be kept or taken in any workroom.

Austria.

No special legislation exists for protecting the health of the workers in the manufacture of china and earthenware.

Potteries are, however, included among works which may not be opened or extended without an official certificate of authorisation, showing that due provision has been made for the security and health of the workers liable to unhealthy influences. In the case of potteries and several other processes and industries, such as chemical works, glass works, &c., the preliminary examination by competent authorities is required to be particularly stringent.

Switzerland.

Instructions for Persons Working in Industries in which Lead and its Compounds are Used.

Prepared by the Inspector of Factories 13th August, 1897.

Dangers arising from work in lead.

The manipulation of lead is injurious to health, as both the metal itself and most of its compounds are poisonous. At the same time, mere occupation in a paint or colour factory where lead is used is not sufficient to induce poisoning, because the materials containing lead must enter the system to produce their toxic effect. The lead can be absorbed by the mouth, the nose, and the skin of the person handling it.

Symptoms of lead poisoning.

The first symptoms of intoxication are failure of appetite, a feeling of weight near the stomach, and constipation. Later on pain in the stomach accompanied by colic results, a condition known as lead colic. On the edge of the gums close to the teeth a greyish blue line appears. The breath becomes foul and the colour of the skin pale and yellowish. If the poisoning continues long enough, rheumatic pains and paralysis, affecting chiefly the hands and forearms, are observed. Sensation may be lost and epileptic fits be induced; the eyes and kidneys also may become seriously affected.

Preventive measures.

All workers are not attacked by lead colic; not because they may not all be rash and imprudent, but because they are not all exposed in the same degree to the poisonous effects. Young persons are more resistant than old. But scrupulous attention to cleanliness is the best preventive.

Although the inhalation of lead dust is injurious, poisoning occurs much less frequently from this source than as the result of the bad habit workpeople have of eating their food and drinking with unwashed hands, or of conveying to their mouth other things covered with dust, such as pipes, cigars, &c.

Negligence of this sort may be continued for a considerable time without obvious evil consequences; and it is just on that account that danger arises, because, by continuing in the practice with more and more boldness, the poison at last becomes concentrated in the system and the poisoning declares itself.

As the dust which enters the mouth and nose sticks mainly to the soft surfaces, it is advisable to frequently wash out the mouth.

This is especially necessary when catarrh of the nose or throat is present, and care should be taken not to swallow the phlegm. An alkaline gargle should be frequently used (e g., a tablespoonful of Carlsbad salts or of soda dissolved in a litre of water). After gargling, it is well to swallow a little of the liquid.

It is absolutely necessary that all who work with lead should wear special clothes or closely fitting blouses, which should be changed or washed every week.

Before each meal the hands should be washed with a brush, soap, and hot water, and the teeth and gums brushed.

Different industries in which lead poisoning may arise.

In places where lead and its compounds are manipulated all processes are dangerous to health, as it is impossible entirely to prevent the hands coming into contact with substances containing lead. It is thus that the following workpeople are exposed to danger:—Painters and varnishers, those laying water and gas pipes, those engaged in jointing metal pipes with red lead containing a high percentage of lead, accumulator works, lapidaries, file-cutters, type-founders, and especially, in the last named industry, those who have to polish the type by the dry method, compositors, gunmakers, and potters employing lead glazes.

Lead colours when moist are harmless.

Attention, however, to cleanliness renders work in moist colours, glazes, enamels,&c.,quite harmless.

In all these varieties of work the hands should be kept clean from the commencement of work, and care should be taken to avoid spilling any of the material. Plumbers should avoid, as far as possible, soiling their clothes; and, above all, never test the efficiency of a joint by applying their lips to the piping. Unfortunately, these precautionary measures, so excessively simple in themselves, are not always observed, because many workpeople find it troublesome to carry on their work with prudence, preferring rough and ready methods, with no thought for the injury such action may bring on themselves and their fellow-workers.

Duties of Managers and Foremen.

Foremen and managers must, therefore, keep a strict supervision over such workpeople, pointing out to them their mistakes, and, if this is unavailing, report them to the occupier. Managers must recognise the responsibility which falls on them of not only looking after the interests of their masters, but also of guarding the health of the operatives.

Every new hand should be placed under the immediate supervision of the manager, and made to work as prescribed in these instructions.

Dry lead colours.

The handling of dried lead compounds causes dust, and consequently all such operations should be carried out with the most scrupulous care to avoid raising dust. Gloves, either of rubber or leather, should be worn on the hands, or vaseline should be rubbed over them. No one should smoke in places where lead is used.

Care in general living.

Predisposition to lead poisoning is much influenced by the habits and home life of the individual. Experience shows that those who are addicted to drink are the first to fall victims. Alcoholic beverages and acid fruits should be avoided, for lead in their presence is rapidly transformed into poisonous salts. Milk and fatty foods are to be recommended.

Cleanliness at home.

Workpeople should be careful not to sleep in the same linen as that worn while at work. Before breakfast, before dinner, and before leaving work, care should be taken to wash thoroughly. The hands and nails should be scrubbed with a brush and soap. Once a week, at least, the workpeople should take a bath. The hair should be kept short.

Medical examination.

In industries where the workers are daily in contact with lead, a periodical examination by a medical man is indispensable.

Once workers have been attacked, it is to their interest to seek some other employment, for relapses take place much more quickly than a first attack.

Recapitulation.

In short, (1) the greatest cleanliness should be observed, and the raising of dust or soiling the hands and clothes should be avoided as far as possible. Smoking and chewing tobacco should be avoided ; (2) overalls, changed every week, should be worn ; (3) no food whatever should be taken in any workroom, but in a special room provided for

Recapitulation. continued. the purpose ; (4) before each meal the mouth should be washed out with warm water and a brush, and the hands washed with warm water and a brush ; (5) once a week, at least, a warm bath should be taken.

(The pottery industry in Switzerland is not very extensive.)

Denmark, Italy, and Norway.

No special legislation exists for the protection of the health of workmen engaged in the manufacture of china or porcelain.

Belgium.

See Professor Thorpe's Report, p. 17.

United States.

The Department of Labour states that there is no legislation, either State or National, especially directed to the giving of expert advice and assistance to manufacturers of pottery relative to the health of the operatives employed. The law which comes nearest to such legislation is an Act passed by the Legislature of the State of Louisiana in 1890. It enacts that the Board of Health may, from time to time, prescribe all needful regulations for the better protection of the health of the operatives and employees working in manufactories, workshops, laboratories, and other places in which substances, materials, or compounds poisonous in their nature or otherwise injurious to the health of the operatives are used, manufactured, compounded, prepared, or handled. Such regulations, when adopted, shall come into force within twenty days after being served by the Board of Health.

Failure to comply with the provisions of the Act is met by a fine of twenty-five dollars or imprisonment for not more than ten days.

Twenty-seven States of the Union have provided in their laws for the establishment of State Boards of Health, one of the duties of which is to investigate the effect of employment upon the public health.